ESSENTIALS OF INTENSIVE INTERVENTION

The Guilford Series on Intensive Instruction
Sharon Vaughn, *Editor*

This series presents innovative ways to improve learning outcomes for K–12 students with challenging academic and behavioral needs. Books in the series explain the principles of intensive intervention and provide evidence-based teaching practices for learners who require differentiated instruction. Grounded in current research, volumes include user-friendly features such as sample lessons, examples of daily schedules, case studies, classroom vignettes, and reproducible tools.

Essentials of Intensive Intervention
*Rebecca Zumeta Edmonds, Allison Gruner Gandhi,
and Louis Danielson*

Intensive Reading Interventions
for the Elementary Grades
*Jeanne Wanzek, Stephanie Al Otaiba,
and Kristen L. McMaster*

Essentials of Intensive Intervention

edited by

Rebecca Zumeta Edmonds
Allison Gruner Gandhi
Louis Danielson

Series Editor's Note by Sharon Vaughn

THE GUILFORD PRESS
New York   London

Library of Congress Cataloging-in-Publication Data

Names: Edmonds, Rebecca Zumeta, editor. | Gandhi, Allison Gruner, editor. |
   Danielson, Louis C., editor.
Title: Essentials of intensive intervention / Edited by Rebecca Zumeta
   Edmonds, Allison Gruner Gandhi, Louis Danielson.
Description: New York, NY : The Guilford Press, [2019] | Series: The Guilford
   series on intensive intervention | Includes bibliographical references and index.
Identifiers: LCCN 2019005037| ISBN 9781462539314 (hardcover : alk. paper) |
   ISBN 9781462539291 (pbk. : alk. paper)
Subjects: LCSH: Learning disabled children--Education (Elementary) | Learning
   disabled children--Education (Secondary) | Behavior modification. |
   Response to intervention (Learning disabled children) | Student assistance programs.
Classification: LCC LC4704.73 .E77 2019 | DDC 371.9/0473--dc23
LC record available at *https://lccn.loc.gov/2019005037*

About the Editors

Rebecca Zumeta Edmonds, PhD, is Principal Researcher at the American Institutes for Research (AIR) in Washington, DC, where she serves as Co-Director of the National Center on Intensive Intervention and as Project Director for an Investing in Innovation and Improvement Development Grant focused on intensive intervention in mathematics. She previously coordinated technical assistance for the Center on Response to Intervention at AIR. A former special education teacher, Dr. Zumeta Edmonds has numerous publications in the areas of response to intervention, multi-tiered systems of support, mathematics intervention, special education policy, implementation, screening, and progress monitoring assessment.

Allison Gruner Gandhi, EdD, is Managing Researcher at AIR in Washington, DC. Since 2005, Dr. Gandhi has led the knowledge development work for the Center on Response to Intervention and the National Center on Intensive Intervention at AIR. In this role, she oversees the development and ongoing maintenance of tools charts that review and rate the technical rigor of screening tools, academic and behavioral progress monitoring tools, and academic and behavioral interventions. She has extensive knowledge about special education policy and practice, especially around identifying and communicating about evidence-based practices to support improved outcomes for students with disabilities.

Louis Danielson, PhD, is Managing Director at AIR in Washington, DC, where he focuses on special education policy and research. He is Senior Advisor to the National Center for Systemic Improvement and Co-Director of the National Center on Intensive Intervention at AIR. A national leader in the field of special education, Dr. Danielson has been involved in programs for students with disabilities since the 1980s. Prior to coming to AIR, he held a leadership role in the U.S. Office for Special Education Programs and was responsible for the Individuals with Disabilities Education Act national activities programs. He also initiated efforts in the U.S. Department of Education that led to widespread adoption of response to intervention.

Contributors

Sarah V. Arden, PhD, Senior Researcher, American Institutes for Research, Seattle, Washington

Tessie Rose Bailey, PhD, Principal Technical Assistance Consultant, American Institutes for Research, Washington, DC

Laura Berry Kuchle, PhD, Senior Researcher, American Institutes for Research, Washington, DC

Gail Chan, PhD, Senior Researcher, American Institutes for Research, Washington, DC

Louis Danielson, PhD, Managing Director, American Institutes for Research, Washington, DC

Douglas Fuchs, PhD, Nicholas Hobbs Chair and Professor of Special Education and Professor of Pediatrics, Peabody College of Vanderbilt University, Nashville, Tennessee

Lynn S. Fuchs, PhD, Dunn Family Chair in Psychoeducational Assessment and Professor of Special Education, Peabody College of Vanderbilt University, Nashville, Tennessee

Allison Gruner Gandhi, EdD, Managing Researcher, American Institutes for Research, Waltham, Massachusetts

Samantha A. Gesel, MEd, Doctoral Candidate, Department of Special Education, Peabody College of Vanderbilt University, Nashville, Tennessee

Steve Goodman, PhD, Director, Michigan's Integrated Behavior and Learning Support Initiative (MIBLSI), Holland, Michigan

Lauren M. LeJeune, MEd, Doctoral Candidate, Department of Special Education, Peabody College of Vanderbilt University, Nashville, Tennessee

Erica S. Lembke, PhD, Professor and Chair, Department of Special Education, University of Missouri, Columbia, Missouri

Christopher J. Lemons, PhD, Associate Professor of Special Education, Peabody College of Vanderbilt University, Nashville, Tennessee

Teri A. Marx, PhD, Senior Researcher, American Institutes for Research, Washington, DC

Jill M. Pentimonti, PhD, Principal Researcher, American Institutes for Research, Washington, DC

Amy Peterson, MA, Senior Researcher, American Institutes for Research, Washington, DC

Jennifer D. Pierce, PhD, Senior Researcher, American Institutes for Research, New York, New York

T. Chris Riley-Tillman, PhD, Professor, Department of Educational, School and Counseling Psychology, University of Missouri, Columbia, Missouri

Rebecca Zumeta Edmonds, PhD, Principal Researcher, American Institutes for Research, Washington, DC

Series Editor's Note

Welcome to the first book in The Guilford Series on Intensive Instruction. As editor for this series, I am particularly excited about *Essentials of Intensive Intervention,* written by a group of outstanding research-to-practice authors led by Rebecca Zumeta Edmonds, Allison Gruner Gandhi, and Louis Danielson, who serve as the critical leadership team for the National Center on Intensive Intervention (NCII; *www.intensiveintervention. org*). This book addresses a pressing need in the field: how we effectively implement evidence-based instruction for students with significant reading and math problems. Many school leaders have embraced response to intervention (RTI)—more recently referred to as multi-tiered systems of support (MTSS)—because it provides an evidence-based framework for screening students early and an ongoing system for monitoring their academic and behavioral progress. Essential to the effective implementation of RTI and MTSS frameworks has been providing effective classroom and instructional practices to remedy students' difficulties. The challenge for many educational stakeholders has been how to address the academic and behavioral concerns of students with the most intensive learning and behavioral needs. This is the first book that thoroughly addresses intensive interventions within an RTI or MTSS model, while also providing very specific and effective guidance on how to implement evidence-based practices to meet the needs of students who require intensive intervention.

Part I of the book addresses data-based individualization (DBI), including a comprehensive overview of DBI and a presentation of issues related to assessment within intensive instructional approaches. Because many students with intensive academic needs also require behavior supports (and vice versa), Part I provides valuable chapters on integrating behavior and academics into intervention planning and delivery and also addresses the needs of youngsters with cognitive disabilities. This is particularly important, since schools have limited time to provide intensive interventions, and mechanisms for integrating behavior and academics may be both more efficient and more effective.

Part II of the book provides specific procedures for DBI implementation and how to individualize data-based decision making. Because DBI implementation often includes a team of school-based individuals (e.g., school psychologist, curriculum leader, teachers, specialists), teaming structures to support intensive intervention using DBI are described, as well as procedures for aligning intensive intervention and special education within MTSS.

The book concludes with a glossary of key terms to help readers understand key ideas and vocabulary.

Most students with intensive academic and behavioral needs do not receive the level and quality of service they require. Teachers and educational leaders are often uninformed about how to adequately address these needs. I am highly enthusiastic about this book, as it offers educational leaders, teachers, and scholars an outstanding, comprehensive source for the research-to-practice knowledge on intensive interventions—both the background essentials and the resources for assessing and implementing effective instruction in schools or classroom. It provides the evidence-based solution in practical ways, including procedures for how to implement effective intensive instruction. Additional features include valuable case studies that illustrate the application of the practices specified. I suspect that many readers will return often to this book, as I know I will.

This volume is a perfect introduction to The Guilford Series on Intensive Instruction. All the books in the series will present innovative ways to improve learning outcomes for K–12 students with challenging academic and behavioral needs. Future books will focus on reading, math, or behavior. As does this first volume, they will provide evidence-based teaching practices for learners who require differentiated instruction and include user-friendly features, such as sample lessons, classroom vignettes, and reproducible tools.

SHARON VAUGHN, PhD

Acknowledgments

We wish to acknowledge the National Center on Intensive Intervention (NCII), which we feature throughout this book. The NCII is funded under the U.S. Department of Education, Office of Special Education Programs, Award No. H326Q160001. Celia Rosenquist serves as the Project Officer. The views expressed in this book do not necessarily represent the positions or policies of the U.S. Department of Education, however. No official endorsement by the U.S. Department of Education of any product, commodity, service, or enterprise mentioned in this volume is intended or should be inferred.

Contents

PART II. IMPLEMENTATION OF DATA-BASED INDIVIDUALIZATION

Purchasers of this book can download and print enlarged versions
of Appendices 1.1 and 7.1 at *www.guilford.com/zumeta-edmonds-forms*
for personal use or use with students (see copyright page for details).

Introduction

Louis Danielson
Rebecca Zumeta Edmonds
Allison Gruner Gandhi

Intensive intervention addresses the needs of students with severe and persistent learning and behavioral challenges, who do not respond to empirically validated interventions that are otherwise effective for most students. Intensive intervention is intended to provide a data-driven, individualized approach to instruction. This book offers a comprehensive overview of intensive intervention and, specifically, one approach to intensive intervention: data-based individualization (DBI). In addition to describing the components of DBI, this book offers practical guidance to those seeking to implement it in their schools. In this introductory chapter, we provide background on the need for intensive intervention, operationalize intensive intervention within the broader framework of a multi-tiered system of support, define DBI, and provide a brief summary of the book's chapters.

THE NEED FOR INTENSIVE INTERVENTION: CHRONICALLY POOR OUTCOMES

In the early 1990s, the U.S. Office of Special Education Programs (OSEP) began reporting the results of the congressionally mandated National Longitudinal Transition Study (NLTS), which provided the first national outcome data that documented relatively poor outcomes for students with disabilities both during secondary school and in their initial years following school. These data indicated significant rates of course failure in high school combined with dropout rates of nearly 40%. Post-high school data reflected low rates of college enrollment and high rates of both unemployment and underemployment (Wagner, Blackorby, Cameto, Hebbeler, & Newman, 1993).

These sobering data were arguably the impetus for what has been a gradual shift in federal focus over the last two decades from procedural compliance with the Individuals with Disabilities Education Act (IDEA) to accountability for improving student outcomes. At the time of the first NLTS reports, no data were available at national or state levels that reported on the academic performance of students with disabilities. Two very important, related events occurred in the mid-1990s to address this issue. First, the National Assessment of Educational Progress (NAEP) began efforts to systematically include students with disabilities, and to report reading and math achievement data for them as a subgroup. In addition, the 1997 reauthorization of IDEA included provisions requiring states and districts to include students with disabilities in their assessments and to also report data separately for them.

The availability of NAEP and statewide assessment data for students with disabilities has helped educators and policymakers to understand both how well these students are doing academically and the extent to which educational improvement efforts have benefited them. The first reports of NAEP performance data in 1996 and 1998 indicated, respectively, that 62% of fourth graders with disabilities were below basic in math, and 75% were below basic in reading. Unfortunately, the period from 1996 until the most recent 2017 NAEP has shown little change in these achievement trends, despite the fact that during the intervening period there have been significant initiatives intended to improve outcomes for students with disabilities. For example, in 2002, Congress enacted the No Child Left Behind legislation (Public Law 107-110, 20 U.S.C. § 6319), which was designed to improve achievement of all students, including those with disabilities. In addition, the OSEP required states to report academic achievement data, and to develop and implement improvement plans. In 2014, the OSEP went even further when it announced a new effort called Results Driven Accountability, which requires that states identify and focus very intently on a particular student-level outcome (e.g., K–3 reading of students with learning disabilities), beginning with a small set of districts and schools, in order to increase the likelihood of success.

Throughout this time period, the OSEP also funded a parallel set of technical assistance projects designed to identify and support implementation of evidence-based approaches for addressing the academic and behavioral needs of students with disabilities. These projects include the National Technical Assistance Center on Positive Behavioral Interventions and Supports (PBIS; 1998–present); the Center on Response to Intervention (CRTI; 2006–2011); the National Center on Intensive Intervention (NCII; 2011–present); and the National Center on Systemic Improvement (NCSI; 2014–present), among others. The work of these centers is particularly important given the broad needs of schools related to implementing multi-tiered systems of support (MTSS), and the more specific challenge for schools to address the needs of students with disabilities for whom efforts to improve achievement have been notably unsuccessful. Given these challenges, the purpose of this book is to help readers understand practices for addressing the needs of students who require the most intensive intervention, most of whom have disabilities, and often do not receive the level of service they require.

INTENSIVE INTERVENTION AND MTSS

We believe intensive intervention, and specifically DBI, is best situated as the most intensive tier, often conceptualized as Tier 3, within MTSS. This is because many of the components of DBI, which you will learn about in later chapters of this book, can be implemented most successfully in schools that have a strong core and supplemental intervention (e.g., Tier 2) program already in place. For example, DBI requires valid, reliable progress-monitoring data to identify students who are not making progress, despite participating in a generally effective Tier 2 intervention. When schools do not have some sort of MTSS in place, accurate identification can be challenging.

The good news is that it appears that there is widespread interest across the country in MTSS. A review of department of education websites for all 50 states and the District of Columbia indicates that every state references initiatives or guidance related to implementation of tiered systems of support (Bailey, 2018). Some states are actively funding statewide initiatives through local or external funding. The Federal Every Student Succeeds Act (ESSA) references "multi-tiered system of support" five times, and permits its use to address K–12 as an allowable use of grant funds [Sec 2224(e)(4)]. Furthermore, ESSA explicitly recognizes MTSS as an approach for improving outcomes for students with disabilities and English language learners [Sec 2103 (b)(3)(F)]. Seven states have included MTSS (or "response to intervention") in their ESSA plans as strategies for ensuring positive outcomes for students with disabilities. This recent reauthorization of ESSA represents the first time that the terms *response to intervention* or *multitiered systems of support* have appeared in federal law or regulation.

You may have noticed a variety of terms that have been used in the education literature to describe tiered systems of support. For example, *response to intervention* (RTI) is often used to describe academically focused frameworks, or procedures used for disability identification, and *positive behavioral interventions and supports* (PBIS) is the term used for multi-tiered systems that address social and behavioral needs in schools. More recently, MTSS has emerged as an alternative term for both RTI and PBIS, and often as a broader term for a system that integrates the two. MTSS reflects a recognition that many students need both academic and behavior interventions and supports; therefore, schools really need a system that integrates planning and delivery of services and support for both of these domains. Regardless of terminology, MTSS frameworks are intended to help schools use data and evidence-based practices to organize service delivery into "tiers" of increasing instructional and intervention intensity.

In this book, we use the term MTSS in the way that it is described in the previous paragraphs and generally avoid using the term RTI. We use the terms Tiers 1, 2, and 3 to mean the following: *Tier 1* refers to core instruction (academics) and the schoolwide behavior management program (behavior); *Tier 2* intervention is the next level of intensity, typically provided for small groups of students who need support in academics or behavior beyond that provided in Tier 1; and *Tier 3* is the most intensive tier for both academics and behavior, and typically involves an individualized plan for a student, although services may be provided to small groups of students. We recognize that some schools may have more than three tiers, but we believe this creates unnecessary complexity and confusion, and can make implementation of MTSS even more challeng-ing. For this reason, we use *Tier 3* to refer to the most intensive level of intervention within MTSS. Although Tier 3 should not exclusively serve students with disabilities, it is often the case that students who require this type of ongoing, individualized support are also students who are receiving special education services. We argue that schools should be integrating services for students with disabilities seamlessly within the larger MTSS system (see Bailey, Chan, & Lembke, Chapter 7, for further discussion).

DATA-BASED INDIVIDUALIZATION

Estimates indicate that approximately 5% of all students fail to respond sufficiently to generally effective, research-validated intervention programs (e.g., Tier 2 or secondary interventions within MTSS). This number corresponds to about 40% of the population of students with disabilities and may include students who are not making adequate progress in their current instructional program or individualized education program (IEP). These students typically present with very low academic achievement even though they might already be receiving specialized services, and they may also exhibit intense or frequent behavior problems.

These students' severe and persistent difficulties suggest that they need an inten-sive intervention; that is, they likely require significant adaptations to intensify their current intervention program to facilitate meaningful progress. The approach to inten-sive intervention that we address in this book is DBI, which is a systemic method for using data to determine when and how to effectively provide more intensive interven-tion to students who need it. The origins of this approach is four decades of research on experimental teaching that was first developed at the University of Minnesota (Deno & Mirkin, 1977) and later expanded upon by others (Capizzi & Fuchs, 2005; Fuchs, Deno, & Mirkin, 1984; Fuchs, Fuchs, & Hamlett, 1989).

As you will learn in more detail later in Chapter 1, the DBI process begins by adapt-ing and intensifying a supplemental, evidence-based intervention program (e.g., a Tier 2 intervention) when a lack of sufficient progress is evident. Teachers then conduct progress monitoring on a weekly basis to determine the student's response. If progress is insufficient, they adapt to intensify the intervention, continuing the progress moni-toring and adaptation cycle until the student responds. While the process is to a degree "trial and error," the adaptations are not random but are instead guided through the intelligent use of formal and informal diagnostic information. And, procedures have also been developed to systematize intensification.

Over the last several years, the team members involved in writing this book have been working with states, districts, and schools to help them implement DBI. In the pro-cess, we have learned several important lessons about what it takes to effectively imple-ment DBI, as well as some of the challenges that implementers often face. For example, we have learned that most schools implementing MTSS are challenged when it comes to implementation at Tier 3. Even schools with well-developed systems for Tiers 1 and 2 are uncertain about how to meet the needs of students who require intensive interven-tion. We have also found that many schools implementing MTSS in both academics and behavior for some time often have some components of Tiers 1 and 2 that are not working well. These have included difficulties charting and using progress-monitoring data, the tendency to use Tier 2 interventions that are not evidenced based, and use of decision rules for Tier 2 services that result in too many students receiving these services. One implication of these challenges is that schools need professional development and ongoing support from trainers and coaches who have deep expertise in components of both DBI *and* MTSS. And perhaps equally importantly, these staff members need to be knowledgeable about *how to implement* systems such as DBI and MTSS.

OVERVIEW OF THE BOOK CHAPTERS

With these considerations in mind, this book is intended to provide an overview of the components of the DBI process, and recommendations for its successful implementation. Part I, The Process of Data-Based Individualization (Chapters 1–4), covers the DBI process, its critical components, and how it may be used to support different groups of students. Part II, Implementation of Data-Based Individualization (Chapters 5–7), addresses factors that may help promote successful implementation of DBI. Each chapter includes key terms, frequently asked questions, and application exercises.

In Chapter 1, Amy Peterson, Louis Danielson, and Douglas Fuchs provide an overview of the five components of the DBI process and its rationale, along with illustrative case examples. They discuss considerations for DBI implementation, including how to identify students for DBI; monitoring fidelity of DBI; and developing a systematic process for intensification. In Chapter 2, Jill M. Pentimonti, Lynn S. Fuchs, and Allison Gruner Gandhi describe screening, progress monitoring, and diagnostic assessment, and explain how each type of assessment is used within DBI. Chapter 3, by Laura Berry Kuchle and T. Chris Riley-Tillman, covers how intervention teams might approach planning for DBI in a manner that addresses both academics and behavior. And in Chapter 4, Christopher J. Lemons, Samantha A. Gesel, and Lauren M. LeJeune discuss how the principles of DBI may be applied to support students with intellectual disabilities.

Part II of this book turns to more practical considerations for implementing DBI. In Chapter 5, Sarah V. Arden and Jennifer D. Pierce address the critical concept of implementation readiness. In Chapter 6, authors Teri A. Marx and Steve Goodman describe how effective use of school teams can support implementation. Finally, in Chapter 7, Tessie Rose Bailey, Gail Chan, and Erica S. Lembke provide recommendations about how to align DBI within a schoolwide MTSS framework and with special education. We also provide a Glossary near the end of the book to help readers understand key terms and vocabulary.

Although we have organized this book so that individual chapters may be read in isolation, we strongly recommend that readers review all the chapters to develop a strong grounding in the critical components of DBI and its implementation. We also recommend that readers begin with Chapter 1 to learn the steps of the DBI process and relevant terminology. Regardless of how you use this book, we hope you find it useful as you prepare to support students with intensive needs to be successful in school. Decades of stagnant, poor outcomes for students with disabilities require a stronger commitment to training school personnel in this evidence-based approach to individualizing instruction for students with intensive needs.

ACKNOWLEDGMENT

We wish to acknowledge the OSEP funding the NCII, which has supported the development of many of the products and resources referenced throughout the book.

REFERENCES

Bailey, T. R. (2018). Is MTSS/RTI here to stay?: All signs point to yes! [National Center on Response to Intervention blog]. Retrieved from *https://rti4success.org/blog/mtssrti-here-stay-all-signs-point-yes*.

Capizzi, A. M., & Fuchs, L. S. (2005). Effects of curriculum-based measurement with and without diagnostic feedback on teacher planning. *Remedial and Special Education, 26*(3), 159–174.

Deno, S. L., & Mirkin, P. K. (1977). *Data-based program modification: A manual.* Reston, VA: Council for Exceptional Children.

Fuchs, L., Deno, S., & Mirkin, P. (1984). The effects of frequent curriculum-based measurement and evaluation on pedagogy, student achievement, and student awareness of learning. *American Educational Research Journal, 21*(2), 449–460.

Fuchs, L. S., Fuchs, D., & Hamlett, C. L. (1989). Effects of instrumental use of curriculum-based measurement to enhance instructional programs. *Remedial and Special Education, 10*(2), 43–52.

Wagner, M., Blackorby, J., Cameto, R., Hebbeler, K., & Newman, L. (1993). *The transition experiences of young people with disabilities: A summary of findings from the National Longitudinal Transition Study of Special Education Students.* Menlo Park, CA: SRI International.

PART I

THE PROCESS OF DATA-BASED INDIVIDUALIZATION

CHAPTER 1

Introduction to Intensive Intervention

A Step-by-Step Guide to Data-Based Individualization

AMY PETERSON
LOUIS DANIELSON
DOUGLAS FUCHS

> **GUIDING QUESTIONS**
>
> ➤ Who needs intensive intervention?
> ➤ What is data-based individualization, and what steps comprise the process?
> ➤ How do I intensify an intervention if my student is not responding to the current approach?
> ➤ How do I know whether I am delivering intensive intervention with fidelity?

To better meet the needs of students with the most severe academic and behavioral needs, often those with disabilities, teachers need to individualize their interventions. For such students, research suggests that simply implementing a new program or delivering more of the same instructional or behavioral approach is not sufficient (Gersten et al., 2009; Kearns & Fuchs, 2013; National Center on Intensive Intervention [NCII], 2013). Implementing an individualized approach is not easy; it demands substantial resources, specific skills and expertise, persistence, and perseverance (D. Fuchs, Fuchs, & Vaughn, 2014). Thus, this approach can only be offered to a relatively small group of students in a school, for example, those who may have participated in a tiered evidence-based intervention program but did not respond adequately, those with very low academic achievement and/or severe behavior problems who are performing poorly in general education classrooms, or those students with disabilities who are not benefiting from their *individualized education programs* (IEPs).

There is no consensus on the number of students who need intensive intervention. Nevertheless, using data from studies on students unresponsive to rigorous supplementary remediation programs (e.g., D. Fuchs, Fuchs, & Compton, 2012; Wanzek & Vaughn,

2009; Conduct Prevention Problems Research Group, 2002), and excluding those who participate in the alternate assessment program, we estimate that about 2.5 million to 5.0 million students (5 to 10% of the general school population) require intensive academic interventions, and approximately 1.5 million students (3% of the general school population) require intensive behavioral interventions. It is important to note that this number may vary by school and the opportunities and resources that young children have been exposed to prior to schooling. As discussed further by Berry Kuchle and Riley-Tillman in Chapter 3, this volume, many students in need of intensive academic or behavioral intervention have co-occurring academic and behavioral challenges (Berry Kuchle, Zumeta Edmonds, Danielson, Peterson, & Riley-Tillman, 2015).

In addition, reviews of implementation of multi-tiered systems of support (MTSS) indicate that even in schools identified as having strong MTSS, response to intervention (RTI), or positive behavioral interventions and supports (PBIS) frameworks in place, teachers face challenges of selecting appropriate assessment tools, linking assessment decisions to instructional decisions, and distinguishing Tier 2 intervention services from intensive intervention for both academics and behavior (e.g., Chafouleas, Volpe, Gresham, & Cook, 2010; Gandhi, Vaughn, Stelitano, Scala, & Danielson, 2015; Kearns, Lemons, Fuchs, & Fuchs, 2014; Severson, Walker, Hope-Doolittle, Kratochwill, & Gresham, 2007; Means, Chen, DeBarger, & Padilla, 2011; Riley-Tillman, Burns, & Gibbons, 2013).

WHAT IS DATA-BASED INDIVIDUALIZATION?

This chapter (and subsequent chapters in this book) introduces an approach to meet the individual needs of these students and to address the challenges outlined earlier. This approach, data-based individualization (DBI), is a systematic and iterative, multistep, evidence-based process that relies on the frequent collection and analysis of student-level data and modification of intervention components when data indicate inadequate response. The DBI process not only helps students struggling primarily with reading, mathematics, and behavior, as well as other content areas, but it also intentionally provides a framework that encourages the integration of academic and behavioral support as appropriate (see Berry Kuchle & Riley-Tillman, Chapter 3, this volume, for more information).

DBI starts when the teacher determines that a student is not making adequate progress and begins to adapt and individualize a standardized intervention based on the specific needs of the student. With DBI, teachers regularly collect data on students' academic performance or school behavior and apply empirically validated decision rules to those data to determine the students' actual response to the intensive instructional (Compton, Fuchs, Fuchs, & Bryant, 2006) or behavior platform (Payne, Scott, & Conroy, 2007). When data indicate that a student is unlikely to achieve the academic or behavioral goal, the teacher experiments by modifying the intervention while continuing to assess the performance or behavior (Vaughn, Denton, & Fletcher, 2010). In this way, the teacher uses the evidence-based DBI process and his or her clinical experience and judgment to adjust the intervention over time to better meet the student's individual needs. DBI is not a quick fix. It is an ongoing process that often requires multiple adaptations over a sustained period of time. In fact, the complexity of acquiring proficiency in reading, writing, and mathematics, as well as background knowledge in the content areas, often requires that students be provided intensive intervention for many years. Decisions about whether and when to reduce the intensity and individualization of the intervention must take into account the student's responsiveness, as well as the breadth and nature of skill deficits to be addressed. While DBI can be implemented by an individual educator (e.g., a special education teacher), it is often implemented through a team-based process that draws expertise from multiple perspectives (e.g., special educators, school psychologists, school counselors, reading, mathematics, or behavioral specialists or interventionists).

The DBI process is not new. Its origins are in a program of research conducted at the University of Minnesota in the 1970s (Deno & Mirkin, 1977), funded by the Office of Special Education Programs in the U.S. Department of Education. Since that time, numerous studies have expanded the research base for DBI and the components of the DBI process (e.g., L. S. Fuchs, Deno, & Mirkin, 1984; L. S. Fuchs, Fuchs, & Hamlett, 1989; Capizzi & Fuchs, 2005; Stecker, Fuchs, & Fuchs, 2005). Specifically, research suggests that DBI can accelerate the performance of many special education students with persistent learning and behavioral difficulties. Randomized controlled trials indicate that its use is associated with moderate-to-large *effect sizes* in reading and mathematics (0.60–1.10; L. S. Fuchs & Fuchs, 1986; Stecker et al., 2005) and behavior change (0.70–0.90; Gresham, 2004).

THE STEPS OF THE DBI PROCESS

Five steps comprise the DBI process, as defined by the NCII (2013). The steps— a *validated intervention program* (Step 1), *progress monitoring* (Step 2), *diagnostic data* (Step 3), *intervention adaptation* (Step 4), and ongoing progress monitoring and adaptation as needed (Step 5)—are outlined in Figure 1.1 and include both interventions (indicated in boxes in the graphic) and assessments or data (indicated in ellipses in the graphic). The following sections describe each of the five steps in more detail.

Step 1: Validated Intervention Program

The validated intervention is typically the same program that was delivered to the students at Tier 2, within an MTSS framework. It is defined as a standardized, evidence-based, academic and/or behavioral intervention (D. Fuchs, Mock, Morgan, & Young, 2003), usually delivered in small groups of students and matched to the group's needs or the function of their behavior and delivered with fidelity. In other words, it is a clearly articulated intervention, with a substantial body of research indicating that it is effective at improving outcomes for most students when delivered as it was designed. The intervention should generally match the critical skills needed by students to achieve

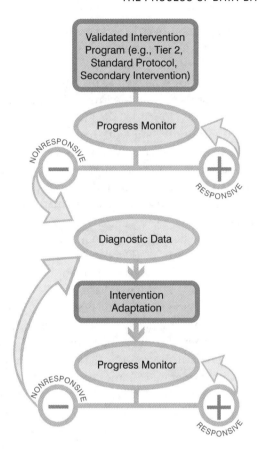

FIGURE 1.1. The iterative steps of the DBI process. Reprinted with permission from the National Center on Intensive Intervention of the American Institutes for Research.

academic success or help them to meet behavioral expectations. There should be procedures in place to ensure that the intervention can be delivered as planned.

This intervention program serves as a "platform" (or starting point) that the teacher will modify to meet students' unique needs through the DBI process. Using a validated intervention program as a base for future adaptations reduces the burden of planning, and it increases the probability that students will learn.

As part of this step, the teacher may make some modifications to intensify the intervention based on what is learned about the students and previous data collected. These modifications may include changing the frequency of the intervention, adjusting the size of the instructional group, or increasing the duration of the intervention session. Changes at this step should not alter the basic intervention and are typically provided to all students in the group.

To determine whether the intervention is a successful approach for the student, teachers collect progress monitoring data along with additional data sources (e.g., fidelity data) throughout the implementation of the intervention program. Analyzing progress monitoring data is the second step in the DBI process.

- **Learn more about validated intervention programs and find relevant tools at** *https://intensiveintervention.org/intensive-intervention/validated-intervention-program.*
- **Selecting or evaluating validated interventions:** The NCII's Academic Intervention Tools Chart (*https://intensiveintervention.org/chart/instructional-intervention-tools*) and Behavioral Intervention Tools Chart (*www.intensiveintervention.org/chart/behavioral-intervention-chart*), along with other repositories such as the What Works Clearinghouse (*https://ies.ed.gov/ncee/wwc*) can help teams select or evaluate the interventions that they are using. The Navigating Evidence-Based Practice Resource Websites Online Module (*http://airhsdlearning.airws.org/ebpwebsites/story_html5.html*) from the National Center for Systemic Improvement can help you to learn how to navigate and evaluate interventions on a number of popular online repositories.

Step 2: Progress Monitoring

Progress monitoring data provide evidence of whether an intervention was successful for a student. At Step 2, the teacher or team of teachers analyzes the progress monitoring data as the teacher implements the intervention program. The teacher collects data using a valid and reliable progress monitoring measure, determines the student's instructional level and baseline, establishes a goal, graphs student progress over time, and measures the student's current rate of progress against the goal using decision rules such as trendline analysis or the four-point rule. Teachers using DBI need to make timely decisions based on a student's progress within intervention. Stecker et al. (2005) and others recommend that for students with intensive needs, teachers monitor students' progress on a weekly basis. Pentimonti, Fuchs, and Ghandi (Chapter 2, this volume) provides a more detailed discussion about features of progress monitoring measures and how progress monitoring data are used to make decisions within the DBI process.

- **Learn more about progress monitoring and find relevant tools at** *https://intensiveintervention.org/intensive-intervention/progress-monitor.*
- **Selecting or evaluating progress monitoring measures:** The NCII's Academic Progress Monitoring Tools Chart (*www.intensiveintervention.org/chart/progress-monitoring*) and Behavioral Progress Monitoring Tools Chart (*www.intensiveintervention.org/chart/behavioral-progress-monitoring-tools*) can help teams select or evaluate their progress monitoring measures. These charts are described in more detail in Pentimonti et al. (Chapter 2, this volume).
- **Analyzing and graphing progress monitoring data:** The NCII's Student Progress Monitoring Tool for Data Collection and Graphing (*https://intensiveintervention.org/resource/student-progress-monitoring-tool-data-collection-and-graphing-excel*) can help teams to graph progress monitoring data and set student goals using different validated goal-setting techniques.

For students whose progress monitoring data indicate that they are responding to the validated intervention, the teacher should continue to provide the intervention and determine when to begin to scale back supports. For students who have not responded adequately to instruction, however, the teacher or team uses diagnostic data to help identify why this has happened and what should be done.

Step 3: Diagnostic Data

At Step 3, the teacher collects diagnostic data to gather more information about the student. Diagnostic data help the teacher to determine why the student has not responded to the intervention and to develop an initial hypothesis. Specifically, diagnostic data, collected with formal and informal measures, may be used to identify patterns that illustrate a student's skills deficits and strengths or the environmental events that predict and maintain the student's problem behavior. At this stage, teachers may rely on the expertise of other members of the team, as well as parents and others who work with the student to enhance the problem-solving process, and should pay particular attention to the interaction between academic and behavioral challenges (see Berry Kuchle & Riley-Tillman, Chapter 3, this volume, for additional information). The diagnostic data and hypothesis drive the team's decisions about how best to support the student and adapt the intervention. Pentimonti et al. (Chapter 2, this volume) provide a more in-depth review of diagnostic measures and how they can be used within the DBI process.

> **Learn more about diagnostic data and find relevant tools at**
> *https://intensiveintervention.org/intensive-intervention/diagnostic-data.*

Step 4: Intervention Adaptation

Using the diagnostic data, the initial hypothesis, and input and expertise of colleagues, the teacher adapts the intervention and develops an individualized intervention plan for the student. The teacher does not make all possible intervention adaptations at once, but prioritizes the adaptations based on the data. The individual intervention plan documents how the intervention should change and is used by the teacher to guide implementation of the adapted intervention.

Adaptations made to intensify the intervention may include a range of strategies but should be supported by student data. Vaughn, Wanzek, Murray, and Roberts (2012) outlined four major areas in which educators can intensify academic interventions: changing the dosage or time; changing the learning environment to promote attention and engagement; combining cognitive processing strategies with academic learning; and modifying the delivery of instruction. Similarly, L. S. Fuchs, Fuchs, and Malone (2017) proposed a taxonomy of intervention intensity that includes the domains of strength, dosage, alignment, attention to transfer, comprehensiveness, behavioral support, and

- **Learn more about intervention adaptations and find relevant resources at** *https://intensiveintervention.org/intensive-intervention/intervention-adaptation.*
- **Individual intervention plans:** The NCII has developed a suite of tools (*https://intensiveintervention.org/implementation-support/tools-support-intensive-intervention-data-meetings*) to help teams facilitate their data meetings and develop individualized intervention plans.
- **Sample lessons and activities:** These sample lessons and activities incorporate explicit instructional principles and practice opportunities to help intensify interventions based on student needs.
  - Math (*https://intensiveintervention.org/intervention-resources/mathematics-strategies-support-intensifying-interventions*)
  - Literacy (*https://intensiveintervention.org/intervention-resources/literacy-strategies*)
  - Behavior (*https://intensiveintervention.org/intervention-resources/behavior-strategies-support-intensifying-interventions*)

individualization to guide continued adaption and intensification based on data. We describe the taxonomy in more detail later in this chapter. Both proposed frameworks and those outlined in other research and expert recommendations (e.g., Gersten et al., 2009; L. S. Fuchs et al., 2008) incorporate common themes, including changes to (1) the available practice and feedback opportunities, (2) the environment, (3) pacing and instructional skills taught, (4) instructional approach employed (e.g., explicit instruction principles), and (5) integration of academic and behavioral supports. All also recommend the ongoing interplay between intervention adaptation and data collection and analysis.

Step 5: Progress Monitoring and the Iterative Nature of DBI

As noted, DBI is an iterative process of data analysis and adaptation. Just as the teacher collects and analyzes progress monitoring data to determine whether the validated intervention implemented in Step 1 was successful, he or she continues to collect and analyze progress monitoring data to determine whether the adaptations they made were successful. On the student's progress monitoring graph the teacher indicates when changes were made to determine which adaptations were more or less successful for the student, and to guide future changes.

If a student responds, the teacher continues to implement the adapted intervention and monitor student progress. If the student does not respond to the adapted intervention, the teacher or team considers whether the intervention was delivered with fidelity and if there are any other factors that may have influenced the student's response. If the teacher identifies potential implementation issues, he or she may continue to collect data to see whether the student will respond if the intervention is delivered as intended. If the teacher does not identify any major implementation issues, the team returns to Step 3, and collects and analyzes diagnostic data to inform additional adaptations over time. The DBI process takes perseverance and persistence. The team members may need to make multiple changes before they find an approach that meets the student's needs. Even when the student makes initial progress, the teacher may find it necessary to revisit the DBI process over time to ensure that the student continues to show improvement.

CONSIDERATIONS FOR IMPLEMENTING DBI

Implementing any intervention, process or approach can be complicated. We introduce in this section some initial areas to consider when implementing DBI, including (1) how to identify students who may need DBI, (2) the importance of monitoring *fidelity of implementation*, (3) how to intensify interventions in a systematic way, (4) whether the DBI process can be implemented in middle and high schools, and (5) the importance of engaging parents and families in the process. Subsequent chapters in the book provide more in-depth implementation guidance around how DBI can be implemented within an MTSS framework (Bailey, Chan, & Lembke, Chapter 7), how you can build effective teams to support implementation (Marx & Goodman, Chapter 6), and how you can prepare for successful DBI implementation (Arden & Pierce, Chapter 5).

Identifying Students Who May Benefit from DBI

As we mentioned previously, because DBI is a time- and resource-intensive process, most schools are unable to implement DBI with a large number of students. Schools may use DBI to support students who have failed to respond to high-quality instruction and evidence-based interventions provided at Tiers 1 or 2, or who present with very low academic achievement or high-frequency or high-intensity behavioral problems. In addition, DBI can support students with disabilities who are not showing adequate progress in their current IEP. If the number of students who need DBI seems too large, teams should review the quality of instruction being delivered at Tiers 1 and 2, including the evidence base and implementation fidelity, before trying to provide DBI (Lemons et al., 2019). Teams may also need to analyze the quality of the collected data to confirm that a technically adequate tool was used, the data were collected consistently, and valid decision rules were implemented.

Considering limitations in resources and differing contexts, there is not an exact science that determines the precise students who need DBI. Teams should consider the available information about the student, interventions that have previously been implemented, and the quality of the data that have been collected to guide their decisions. To collect this information, teams may use or adapt the Premeeting Background Form (see Appendix 1.1) developed by the NCII to help them prepare for the initial meeting.

Monitoring Fidelity of Implementation within the DBI Process

Fidelity refers to whether the prescribed procedures are followed. In the case of DBI, this includes fidelity to the intervention, assessments, decision-making processes, and implementation plans. When interventions and assessments are implemented with fidelity, teams make more accurate decisions about an individual student's progress and future intervention needs. In addition, fidelity of implementation to the DBI process across multiple students in a school helps to ensure that staff members have the necessary resources and processes in place to support strong implementation for individual students.

What Does It Mean for an Intervention to Be Delivered with Fidelity?

In simple terms, this is an assessment of the extent to which you have done what you set out to do. In other words, all elements of content are covered, and the session frequency, duration, and group size are consistent with what is recommended. At Tier 2, this means following the recommendations outlined and studied by the intervention developer. When adaptations are made as part of the DBI process, this means following the individualized intervention plan that was developed by the team based on the student's data. If the fidelity of intervention is not clearly monitored, and the student does not respond sufficiently, it can be difficult to determine whether the student truly needs DBI and whether the changes that were made as part of the DBI process were successful or unsuccessful.

> The NCII has developed the Data-Based Individualization Implementation Log: Daily and Weekly Intervention Review (*https://intensiveintervention.org/resource/ dbi-implementation-log-daily-and-weekly-intervention-review*) that allows teachers to monitor fidelity of implementation to the intervention being provided and to take note of any potential challenges and the student's engagement in the intervention. Together these can be helpful when making decisions about future changes that are needed.

What Does It Mean to Monitor Progress with Fidelity?

Just as it is important for teachers to consider whether they have implemented the intervention with fidelity, they must also consider whether the progress monitoring measures were delivered consistently over time. Limiting variability in how the assessment is administered, scored, and the decision-making process, helps to ensure that progress or lack thereof clearly represents a student's response to the instruction and intervention rather than other variables. Aspects of consistency that should be considered include (1) use of the same progress monitoring system; (2) progress monitoring at the same instructional level; (3) applying consistent administrative procedures; and (4) using consistent scoring procedures. For example, changing the environment or the way directions or feedback are provided may influence the student's response and add confounding variables, so that it becomes impossible to disentangle whether the changes in student progress are related to the intervention or to the change in location, or to the directions or feedback the student received when completing the progress monitoring assessment. At the same time, there may be factors that are outside your control. For example, a student's score may fluctuate after an extended holiday vacation, absence, medication change, or due to stress at home. It is important to take note of these potential variables and consider the factors that may have impacted the student's response when making instructional decisions based on their data.

What Does It Mean to Monitor Fidelity of the DBI Process?

For schools and districts that are implementing DBI across multiple students, it is important to consider the fidelity to implementation of the process at the team and school levels. This includes bringing together information about the implementation of interventions, assessments, and decision-making processes across multiple students. Reviewing these data can help teams plan where they need to target resources and supports, in order to address potential barriers and plan next steps.

Information about readiness and implementation is discussed further by Arden and Pierce (Chapter 5, this volume).

The NCII has developed a number of tools that can be used by teams when monitoring fidelity. These include:

- The Data Meeting Plan Fidelity Checklist (*https://intensiveintervention.org/resource/data-meeting-plan-fidelity-checklist*) that helps teams monitor how their data meetings are being implemented to develop individualized intervention plans and monitor student progress.
- The Student Level Plan Fidelity Checklist (*https://intensiveintervention.org/resource/student-level-plan-fidelity-checklist*) that helps teams review documents and improve implementation of DBI for a group of students they serve.
- The DBI Implementation Rubric and Interview (*https://intensiveintervention.org/resource/dbi-implementation-rubric-and-interview*) that monitors school-based implementation of DBI and the structures and supports necessary to implement DBI successfully.

Developing a Systematic Process for Intensifying Interventions

When considering the validated intervention program and the adaptations to the intervention, teachers benefit from paying attention to a series of instructional features: strength, dosage, alignment, attention to transfer, comprehensiveness, behavioral support, and individualization. These dimensions are part of *taxonomy of intervention intensity* defined by L. S. Fuchs et al. (2017) and are briefly defined in Table 1.1.

The dimensions of the taxonomy (L. S. Fuchs et al., 2017) should help teachers to determine the strengths and weakness of different interventions and guide decisions about how to adjust the intervention to better meet students' needs. All interventions have strengths and weaknesses. Thus, teachers should use their knowledge of students and their academic and behavioral areas of need to determine dimensions that are most important and prioritize changes based on this knowledge.

TABLE 1.1. Taxonomy of Intervention Intensity Dimensions

Strength. How well the intervention has been shown to be successful for students with intensive needs. More specifically, did the developers of the intervention provide outcome data specifically for students with intensive needs (typically those below the 20th percentile) and were the effects of the intervention for those students substantial enough to have practical value?

Dosage. The number of opportunities the student has to respond and receive feedback from the teacher. This includes the number of sessions, length of sessions (minutes per session), as well as number of participants in the session. It also includes the structure of the lesson and the times during the lessons that the student might be able to respond and receive feedback. For student behavior, this includes the number of opportunities that the student has to receive positive feedback for an appropriate behavior and corrective feedback for behavior concerns.

Alignment. How well the intervention matches the targeted academic skills or the behaviors of concern, as well as incorporates grade-appropriate standards or the behaviors that are expected for a particular context (i.e., Tier 1 or schoolwide context).

Attention to transfer. Whether the intervention is explicitly designed to help students make connections between the skills taught in the intervention and skills learned in other contexts and environments. For student behavior, this focuses on the extent to which an intervention generalizes to an increase in appropriate behaviors or to a decrease in behaviors of concern across contexts and time.

Comprehensiveness. Whether the intervention incorporates a comprehensive array of explicit instruction principles (e.g., providing explanations in simple, direct language; modeling efficient solution strategies instead of expecting students to discover strategies on their own; ensuring that students have the necessary background knowledge and skills to succeed with those strategies; gradually fading support for students' correct execution of those strategies; providing practice so students use the strategies to generate many correct responses; and incorporating systematic cumulative review).

Behavior or academic support. For students struggling academically, the behavior support dimension considers whether an academic intervention incorporates behavioral strategies that may support students with self-regulation, motivation, or with externalizing behaviors that may impact their ability to learn. For behavior, the academic support dimension considers the academic components that may be included or referenced within a behavioral intervention.

Individualization. The ongoing use of progress monitoring data and other diagnostic data sources to intensify and individualize the intervention based on student need. In this way, individualization closely maps to a number of steps in the DBI process outlined in this chapter. This includes the collection of progress monitoring (Step 2) and diagnostic data (Step 3); the ongoing modification of instruction (Step 4), and the continuous data collection and repetition of this process until improvement is shown (Step 5).

Implementing DBI at the Middle or High School Level

While the components of the DBI process may be applied across grade levels, challenges occur with implementation at the later grades due to lack of valid and reliable assessment tools or evidence-based standard protocol interventions. In addition, schools may need to consider additional factors related to scheduling, teacher expertise, and teaming processes. Subsequent chapters in this volume address some of these challenges and suggest ways to support implementation at the secondary level.

Engaging Parents and Families within the DBI Process

Parents and families play a critical role in supporting the DBI process, but it is important to recognize that every parent and family member is different, with varying levels of knowledge and levels of comfort with school. To support the DBI process, parents and families can share information that the school and teacher may not be aware of and may provide instructional support and reinforcement at home. Teams should share information about the DBI process and intensive intervention with parents and families, and encourage them to share information about their student. They may invite parents to be involved in meetings, provide strategies that can be used at home, and share progress monitoring data. NCII has developed a series of resources to support families in learning more about DBI and intensive intervention. These are available on the NCII website (*www.intensiveintervention.org/implementation-support/collaborating-families*).

CASE EXAMPLE

This section provides an example of DBI in action. While in practice, DBI is a complex, ongoing, and iterative process, this fictitious example provides a simpler version of the DBI process to illustrate the steps of the process.

Ms. Johnson, a special education teacher at Deerfield Elementary School, was concerned that some students on her caseload were failing to meet their IEP goals and were not showing adequate progress in their current intervention program. She had previously worked at a school that provided intensive intervention using the DBI process and thought it would be helpful at Deerfield. She noticed that the school already had a good foundation that included access to a valid and reliable progress monitoring tool and a range of evidence-based interventions.

With the support of the leadership team, Ms. Johnson decided to pilot the DBI process with Monica, a third-grade student who had previously received Tier 2 interventions during second grade, and was diagnosed with a learning disability in reading following a comprehensive evaluation. To initiate the DBI process, Ms. Johnson and a team discussed Monica's data and the previous supports she had received, and decided that the DBI process would help them to develop a better IEP both to meet Monica's needs and to address her lack of response to the current intervention. Ms. Johnson also talked with Monica's family to identify areas of concern and to ensure that they understood the process. Specifically, Ms. Johnson shared three one-page handouts from NCII that provided an overview of intensive intervention, shared questions that parents and families might want to ask, and offered tips for supporting Monica at home (view the handouts at *www. intensiveintervention.org/resource/intensive-intervention-infographics-parents-and-families*).

The team used the dimensions of the taxonomy of intervention intensity to consider a starting point for Monica's intervention. One of the areas that the team was interested in learning about was the evidence base or strength of the current intervention that was being used with Monica. To find this information, the team reviewed the Academic Intervention Tools Chart from NCII (*www.intensiveintervention.org/chart/instructional-intervention-tools*). Ms. Johnson explained to the team that the Academic Intervention Tools Chart reviews studies of interventions and that these reviews are completed by a panel of experts. She illustrated that the chart is interactive and provides information related to study quality, study results, intensity, and additional research.

> **APPLICATION EXERCISE 1.1. Exploring the Academic Intervention Tools Chart**
>
> Review the Academic Intervention Tools Chart (*www.intensiveintervention.org/chart/instructional-intervention-tools*). Click on each of the tabs in the chart, try the filters, and click on the bubbles on the chart front to explore the comprehensive information available on the charts. Using the information on the charts, address the following:
>
> 1. Identify the available reading interventions for elementary students on the chart that provide partially convincing or convincing ratings for at least four areas of study quality.
> 2. How many of those studies have evidence of substantive results (results with an effect size greater than 0.25 as defined by What Works Clearinghouse [2017]) for measures the intervention directly targeted as a focus (noted on the chart as Targeted Measures) *and* provide disaggregated data for students below the 20th percentile?
> 3. Of those that you have identified in item 2, find the information about the dosage (frequency of intervention sessions, number of minutes per session, and number of weeks in intervention) required to implement one intervention.

After reviewing the tools chart, the team was pleased that the intervention that Monica had been receiving showed strong effects for the population of students below the 20th percentile and incorporated an extensive focus on explicit instruction and strategies for self-regulation and executive function. Because Monica's data indicated that she was making some progress in the intervention, but that it was not adequate to meet her end-of-year goal, the team decided to intensify the intervention by decreasing the number of students in the intervention group and providing 15 additional minutes of instruction a day (increasing the dose). The team made this decision because it provided Monica with more opportunities to respond and to get feedback from Ms. Johnson, and it decreased the likelihood of distraction from other students. Ms. Johnson collected progress monitoring data on a weekly basis and used NCII's DBI Implementation Log (*www.intensiveintervention.org/resource/dbi-implementation-log-daily-and-weekly-intervention-review*) to monitor fidelity.

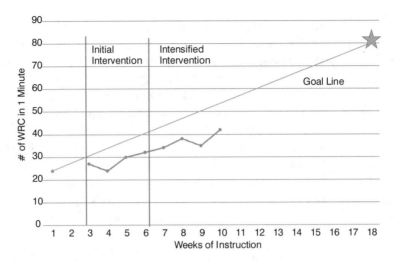

FIGURE 1.2. Graph of Monica's weekly progress monitoring data, measured in words read correctly (WRC) per minute for the initial intervention and the intensified intervention. Goal line = 80 WRC per minute after 18 weeks.

After 4 weeks, the team reconvened to discuss Monica's progress. At that time, they reviewed the progress monitoring data and determined how Monica was responding to the intervention (see Figure 1.2).

APPLICATION EXERCISE 1.2. Has Monica Responded to the Intervention?

Answer the following using the graph provided:

1. Did Monica respond to the intervention that Ms. Johnson provided?
2. What additional questions might the team have when looking at Monica's graph?
3. What might they do next?

After reviewing the data, the team determined that Monica was not on track to meet her goal. They pointed out that all of Monica's data points were below her goal line. Having reviewed the graphed progress monitoring data, the team wanted to confirm that there were no issues with the implementation of the intervention. The fidelity log data indicated that there were no issues with implementation. Ms. Johnson provided the intervention as intended, for the required length, and Monica was typically highly engaged in the intervention.

To inform the intervention change, Ms. Johnson conducted a miscue analysis of Monica's progress monitoring data and a decoding skills inventory. Based on the results, the team increased the time spent on decoding vowel team words in and out of context and introduced an audio recording activity. Ms. Johnson continued to collect and graph progress monitoring data and the team met to review Monica's progress.

The NCII website (*www.intensiveintervention.org*) has a wealth of resources focused on DBI and the steps of the DBI process. These include:

- Self-Paced Learning Module: Introduction to Intensive Intervention (*https://intensiveintervention.org/resource/self-paced-introduction-intensive-intervention*)
- IRIS Star Legacy Modules:
  - Intensive Intervention (Part 1): Using Data-Based Individualization to Intensify Instruction (*https://iris.peabody.vanderbilt.edu/module/dbi1/#content*)
  - Intensive Intervention (Part 2): Collecting and Analyzing Data for Data-Based Individualization (*https://iris.peabody.vanderbilt.edu/module/dbi2/#content*)
- Data-Based Individualization: A Framework for Intensive Intervention (*https://intensiveintervention.org/resource/data-based-individualization-framework-intensive-intervention*)

Because Monica did not respond as expected to the adaptations, the team conducted additional diagnostic assessment to further refine and individualize the intervention for Monica. This continuous process ensured that Monica's unique learning needs were being addressed.

SUMMARY

For students with severe and persistent learning needs, the DBI process serves as an ongoing cycle of data analysis and adaptation. While DBI relies on components of instruction and data collection that are already present in many schools, particularly those implementing MTSS, the process demands a systematic, research-based approach and requires skilled educators to collect, analyze, and review data; to adapt interventions by increasing their intensity and individualization; and to persist over time. The following chapters of this book expand on the DBI process and describe considerations for implementation within an MTSS context.

FREQUENTLY ASKED QUESTIONS

What are some of the implementation considerations for supporting DBI within a school?

Strong school leadership, schedules that allow for intervention delivery and regular data team meetings, availability of valid and reliable progress monitoring measures and evidence-based interventions, systematic and established processes and procedures to facilitate team meetings, and staff with the skills and expertise to collect and analyze data and refine and adapt interventions are all essential for the effective implementation of DBI. Chapters 5–7 provide additional information and details about considerations for implementing DBI within an MTSS framework (Bailey et al., Chapter 7), the role of teams supporting DBI (Marx & Goodman, Chapter 6), and readiness (Arden & Pierce, Chapter 5).

How does DBI fit within an MTSS framework?

The DBI process does not occur in isolation. Rather, it is part of a continuum of instruction and intervention often provided through an MTSS framework. DBI is a more intensive intervention option than the instruction and interventions provided at Tiers 1 and 2. Because DBI does not exist in a vacuum, its success is connected with the success of other tiers in the framework. For example, the fidelity with which Tiers 1 and 2 are implemented sets the foundation for successful implementation of DBI. Additionally, DBI may be used for students who require intensive intervention in one subject area (e.g., math) but receive Tier 1 or Tier 2 in other areas (e.g., literacy). Subsequent chapters in this book, including Chapters 5–7, provide a more in-depth review of the implementation of DBI within a MTSS framework.

Is DBI the same as special education? Is DBI only provided by special educators?

In the case example in this chapter, Monica is a student with a reading disability, and Ms. Johnson is a special education teacher who used DBI to intensify the supports provided to Monica. This case illustrates how DBI can enhance the quality of special education services by providing teachers a systematic data-based process for the following:

- Delivering specially designed instruction based on student need.
- Writing ambitious but realistic IEP goals.
- Evaluating progress toward IEP goals.
- Intensifying specialized instruction for students who are not making adequate progress.
- Planning for the whole child.

In addition, Lemons et al. (Chapter 4, this volume) provide information about how DBI can be used to support students with intellectual disabilities.

While these cases show how DBI can be applied to support students with disabilities, special education alone should not assume the responsibility of conducting DBI, and DBI will not be necessary for every student with a disability. Historically, special educators have been trained and responsible for supporting the most difficult-to-teach students, including those with intensive academic and behavioral needs. Because of this, and because many students who require DBI are students with disabilities, special educators are well positioned to use the DBI process to support these students. However, DBI often requires collaborative problem solving that incorporates multiple perspectives and roles. In this way, schools gather input from multiple staff members and determine who is the most qualified to address students' needs, including, but not limited to, special educators.

REFERENCES

Berry Kuchle, L., Zumeta Edmonds, R., Danielson, L. C., Peterson, A., & Riley-Tillman, T. C. (2015). The next big idea: A framework for integrated academic and behavioral intensive intervention. *Learning Disabilities Research and Practice, 30,* 150–158.

Capizzi, A. M., & Fuchs, L. S. (2005). Effects of curriculum-based measurement with and without diagnostic feedback on teacher planning. *Remedial and Special Education, 26*(3), 159–174.

Chafouleas, S. M., Volpe, R. J., Gresham, F. M., & Cook, C. R. (2010). Behavioral assessment within problem-solving models: Current status and future directions. *School Psychology Review, 39,* 343–349.

Compton, D. L., Fuchs, D., Fuchs, L. S., & Bryant, J. D. (2006). Selecting at-risk readers in first grade for early intervention: A two-year longitudinal study of decision rules and procedures. *Journal of Educational Psychology, 98*(2), 394–409.

Conduct Prevention Problems Research Group. (2002). Evaluation of the first 3 years of the Fast Track prevention trail with children at high risk for adolescent conduct problems. *Journal of Abnormal Child Psychology, 30*(1), 19–35.

Deno, S. L., & Mirkin, P. K. (1977). *Data-based program modification: A manual.* Minneapolis, MN: Leadership Training Institute for Special Education.

Fuchs, D., Fuchs, L. S., & Compton, D. (2012). Smart RTI: A next-generation approach to multi-level prevention. *Exceptional Children, 78*(3), 263–279.

Fuchs, D., Fuchs, L. S., & Vaughn, S. (2014). What is intensive instruction and why is it important? *Teaching Exceptional Children, 46*(4), 13–18.

Fuchs, D., Mock, D., Morgan, P. L., & Young, C. (2003). Responsiveness-to-intervention: Definitions, evidence, and implications for the learning disabilities construct. *Learning Disabilities Research and Practice, 18*(3), 157–171.

Fuchs, L. S., Deno, S. L., & Mirkin, P. K. (1984). Effects of frequent curriculum-based measurement of evaluation on pedagogy, student achievement, and student awareness of learning. *American Educational Research Journal, 21,* 449–460.

Fuchs, L. S., & Fuchs, D. (1986). Effects of systematic formative evaluation: A meta-analysis. *Exceptional Children, 53*(3), 199–208.

Fuchs, L. S., Fuchs, D., & Hamlett, C. L. (1989). Effects of instrumental use of curriculum-based measurement to enhance instructional programs. *Remedial and Special Education, 10,* 43–52.

Fuchs, L. S., Fuchs, D., & Malone, A. (2017). The taxonomy of intervention intensity. *Teaching Exceptional Children, 50*(1), 35–43.

Fuchs, L. S., Fuchs, D., Powell, S. R., Seethaler, P. M., Cirino, P. T., & Fletcher, J. M. (2008). Intensive intervention for students with mathematics disabilities: Seven principles of effective practice. *Learning Disability Quarterly, 31,* 79–92.

Gandhi, A. G., Vaughn, S., Stelitano, L., Scala, J., & Danielson, L. (2015). Lessons learned from district implementation of intensive intervention: A focus on students with disabilities. *Journal of Special Education Leadership, 28*(1), 39–49.

Gersten, R., Compton, D., Connor, C. M., Dimino, J., Santoro, L., Linan-Thompson, S., & Tilly, W. D. (2009). *Assisting students struggling with reading: Response to intervention and multi-tier intervention for reading in the primary grades: A practice guide* (NCEE 2009-4045). Washington, DC: National Center for Education Evaluation and Regional Assistance, Institute of Education Sciences, U.S. Department of Education. Retrieved from *http://ies.ed.gov/ncee/wwc/publications/practiceguides.*

Gresham, F. (2004). Current status and future directions of school-based behavioral interventions. *School Psychology Review, 33,* 326–343.

Kearns, D., & Fuchs, D. (2013). Does cognitively focused instruction improve the academic performance of low-achieving students? *Exceptional Children, 79*(3), 263–290.

Kearns, D. M., Lemons, C. J., Fuchs, D., & Fuchs, L. S. (2014). Essentials of a tiered intervention system to support unique learners: Recommendations from research and practice. In J. Mascolo, D. Flanagan, & V. Alfonso (Eds.), *Essentials of planning, selecting, and tailoring interventions for the unique learner* (pp. 56–91). Hoboken, NJ: Wiley.

Lemons, C. J., Sinclair, A. C., Gesel, S., Gandhi, A. G., & Danielson, L. (2019). Integrating intensive intervention into special education services: Guidance for special education administrators. *Journal of Special Education Leadership, 32*(1).

Means, B., Chen, E., DeBarger, A., & Padilla, C. (2011). *Teachers' ability to use data to informal instruction: Challenges and supports.* Washington, DC: U.S. Department of Education. Retrieved from *http://files.eric.ed.gov/fulltext/ed516494.pdf.*

National Center on Intensive Intervention. (2013). *Data-based individualization: A framework for intensive intervention.* Washington, DC: Office of Special Education, U.S. Department of Education.

Payne, L. D., Scott, T. M., & Conroy, M. (2007). A school-based examination of the efficacy of function-based intervention. *Behavioral Disorders, 32,* 158–174.

Riley-Tillman, T. C., Burns, M. K., & Gibbons, K. (2013). *RTI applications: Vol. 2. Assessment, analysis, and decision making.* New York: Guilford Press.

Severson, H. H., Walker, H. M., Hope-Doolittle, J., Kratochwill, T. R., & Gresham, F. M. (2007). Proactive, early screening to detect behaviorally at-risk students: Issues, approaches, emerging innovations, and professional practices. *Journal of School Psychology, 45,* 193–223.

Stecker, P. M., Fuchs, L. S., & Fuchs, D. (2005). Using curriculum-based measurement to improve student achievement: Review of research. *Psychology in the Schools, 42,* 795–819.

Vaughn, S., Denton, C. A., & Fletcher, J. M. (2010). Why intensive interventions are necessary for students with severe reading difficulties. *Psychology in the Schools, 47,* 432–444.

Vaughn, S., Wanzek, J., Murray, C. S., & Roberts, G. (2012). *Intensive interventions for students struggling in reading and mathematics: A practice guide.* Portsmouth, NH: RMC Research Corporation, Center on Instruction.

Wanzek, J., & Vaughn, S. (2009). Students demonstrating persistent low response to reading intervention: Three case studies. *Learning Disabilities Research and Practice, 24*(3), 151–163.

What Works Clearinghouse. (2017). *Procedures handbook version 4.0.* Washington, DC: Institute of Educational Sciences, U.S. Department of Education. Retrieved from *https://ies.ed.gov/ncee/wwc/docs/referenceresources/wwc_procedures_handbook_v4.pdf.*

Premeeting Background Form

Directions: *The referring teacher should complete this form and submit it to the facilitator at least 1 week before the initial meeting.*

Team Information	
Teacher completing form:	Date:
Service providers (list names and roles):	

Student Information		
Student name:	Parent/guardian:	Parent/guardian contact info:
Teacher:	Grade:	DOB:

IEP or 504 plan? _____ If the student has an IEP or 504 plan, who is the case manager? _____	If the student has an IEP or 504 plan, has the case manager been invited to the meeting? _____	Is the student an English language learner? _____	Has the student had a recent hearing and vision screening? _____ Results?
Has there been consistent communication with the parent/guardian? _____ Will he or she attend the meeting? _____		If the referring teacher is not the general educator, has there been consistent communication with the classroom teacher/general educator? _____ Will he or she attend the meeting? _____	

(continued)

Reprinted with permission from the National Center on Intensive Intervention at the American Institutes for Research.

Current Supports	
Content area *(Check all that apply.)*	**Describe current supports and tier of intervention/support (if applicable).**
☐ Reading ☐ Mathematics ☐ Behavior/social skills ☐ Other	

Current Intervention Program *(Complete this section for each intervention in the primary area of concern that has been previously attempted.)*			
Description of intervention program:		**Intervention provider:**	
Minutes per session:	**Sessions per week:**	**Group size:**	**Setting:**

Intervention implementation considerations: Has the intervention been delivered as planned? Have any challenges or barriers prevented the student from receiving the intervention (e.g., scheduling, behavior, absences)?

Progress monitoring tool or measure (including unit or type of score, such as words per minute, frequency tallies of behavior):	**Frequency of progress monitoring:**	**Goal (must be quantifiable):**
Is the student on track to meet the goal?	**Progress monitoring graph:** *(Attach graphed data, if available.)*	

How is the student performing relative to others in the intervention group? Describe.

(continued)

Premeeting Background Form *(page 3 of 3)*

Student Performance Summary *(Describe student performance in relevant content areas only, including strengths and areas of concern.)*	
Content area *(Check all that apply.)*	**Describe strengths and challenges.**
☐ Reading ☐ Mathematics ☐ Behavior/social skills ☐ Other	
Describe motivators/preferences.	

Student Data Summary			
Hypothesized skill deficit or function of behavior: *(Describe below or provide relevant documents.)*			
State or district standardized assessment scores:	**Behavior data from district data system (e.g., office disciplinary referrals [ODRs] from current year or historical ODR data):**	**Attendance for current year (and historical data when applicable):**	**Current grades:**
Work samples that illustrate area of concern (diagnostic or formative assessments): *(List the attached documents.)*		**Screening data (including student score and norm in each area):**	

CHAPTER 2

Issues of Assessment within Intensive Intervention

JILL M. PENTIMONTI
LYNN S. FUCHS
ALLISON GRUNER GANDHI

GUIDING QUESTIONS

> How do I know that my student needs intensive intervention?

> How can assessment help me understand how to individualize instruction to address my student's unique needs?

> How do I know that I am using the right assessment tool?

> How often should I be assessing my student?

Assessment is an essential part of the data-based individualization (DBI) process. As described by Peterson, Danielson, and Fuchs (Chapter 1, this volume), DBI is a five-step, iterative process that involves ongoing use of data to adjust instruction to meet a student's individual needs. DBI is used with students who demonstrate the most intensive needs and is often implemented within a broader multi-tiered system of support (MTSS) framework that varies the intensity of instruction in accordance with increasing levels of student need. Assessment is critical at all levels of MTSS, and most especially for DBI. Without technically strong assessment, which provides accurate, meaningful information, a teacher has no objective method for determining what the student needs or how to intensify instruction to meet those needs. The close connection between assessment and intervention is at the foundation of the DBI process, because it is what drives the teacher's decision making. With the right assessment tools and guidance on how to use them, teachers can make sound, data-based decisions about *who* needs intensive intervention, *when* to make instructional changes, and *what* skills to focus on.

Assessment is a broad term that encompasses different types used for different purposes. When implementing DBI, assessment is typically used for three purposes:

(1) screening; (2) progress monitoring; and (3) diagnosis of instructional or behavior support needs. *Screening* is often associated with the term *universal screening*, which is conducted with all students in a school to identify who may be at risk and in need of secondary (or Tier 2) intervention. It is not typically used to identify students in need of intensive intervention. However, accurate schoolwide screening procedures are critical for setting the foundation for a successful tiered system of support and for understanding student risk levels. And, in some cases, screening data may be used to identify students who need to move immediately into intensive intervention rather than proceed in lockstep fashion through the levels of support embedded within an MTSS framework (see Al Otaiba, Wagner, & Miller, 2014). Additionally, schools often purchase suites of assessment tools (e.g., AIMSweb, DIBELS) that can be used for both screening and progress monitoring. Implementers of DBI must therefore understand the difference between using these tools for these different purposes.

When the purpose is *progress monitoring*, assessment is used to measure growth for students, specifically those already identified as being at risk for poor learning outcomes. Regular collection of student growth toward a year-end or semester-end learning objective and systematic analysis of those data can inform teachers about whether a student is on track to meet predetermined goals. Using clear decision rules provided by the progress monitoring assessment, teachers know when they should make changes to their instructional plans. Finally, using assessment for *diagnosis* allows teachers to identify specific skills or strategies they need to address when making changes to the instructional program. In this chapter, we provide more detailed descriptions of each of these types of assessment, including examples at the elementary grades. We then describe three important considerations for implementing assessment for DBI: (1) selecting a screening or progress monitoring tool; (2) analyzing progress monitoring data; and (3) functioning in the middle and high school context. Finally, we provide a brief summary, along with a set of application exercises.

SCREENING

Teachers conduct screening to identify the subset of their students who are unlikely to profit from the general education program, unless they receive supplemental instruction. Although screening is not one of the steps in the DBI process, it is the first step within the MTSS context to understanding which students may be at risk of academic failure. The goal of screening is to provide this subset of students with prevention services (i.e., secondary prevention, or Tier 2 intervention) as quickly as possible, before they experience failure. The hope is that the timely provision of short-term prevention services will give them the academic boost they require to then succeed in the general education program, with strong long-term academic outcomes, thereby avoiding the chronic and severe difficulties that students with disabilities often face throughout school and in their adult lives. Screening may also be used to identify students whose needs are so severe that they would benefit from receiving intensive intervention right away (Al Otaiba et al., 2014).

With screening, schools typically assess all students in the school at one point in time, usually near the beginning of the school year, on a brief test. (Some schools also conduct screening midyear and again near the end of the school year.) The screening tool provides a cut point for identifying at-risk students; the cut point is the score on the test below which students are deemed at-risk for poor long-term outcomes in that academic domain. Many screening tests are forms of curriculum-based measurement (CBM), which make good screening instruments because the tests are usually brief and, as a form of general outcome measurement (explained below), they typically provide strong technical data indicating that the test scores are accurate and meaningful indicators of overall performance in the academic domain. We next provide an example of a reading and a math CBM screening tool at first grade.

With CBM Word Identification Fluency (L. S. Fuchs, Fuchs, & Compton, 2004), students are presented with a list of 50 words randomly sampled from 100 high-frequency preprimer, primer, and first-grade words (see Figure 2.1 for an example list). Students read as many of these words as they can in 1 minute, and their scores represent the number read correctly during that minute. If a student finishes in less than 1 minute, the score is prorated. Usually, two alternative forms of CBM Word Identification Fluency (each with a different set of 50 words randomly selected from the same corpus of high-frequency preprimer, primer, and first-grade words) are administered in one sitting. The child's score is the average across both alternative forms, so screening takes approximately 3 minutes per child. Students whose average score falls below 10 words read correctly (near the start of first grade) are considered at risk for poor long-term reading outcomes. In many schools, scoring below the screening test's cut point provides the basis for secondary (Tier 2) intervention. We return to this point below.

In mathematics, CBM Calculations and CBM Concepts and Applications (also known as Monitoring Basic Skills Progress; Fuchs, Hamlett, & Fuchs, 1990) are often used together as a first-grade screening tool to identify students who are at risk for poor long-term mathematics outcomes. CBM Calculations is a 25-item test that samples the typical first-grade calculations curriculum: adding two single-digit numbers (9 items), subtracting two single-digit numbers (10 items), adding three single-digit numbers (2 items), adding two two-digit numbers without regrouping (2 items), and subtracting a single-digit number from a two-digit number (2 items). Students have 2 minutes to complete as many items as possible (see Figure 2.2 for an example test). CBM Calculations is administered in whole-class format. The classroom teacher passes out the CBM Calculations Test face down. The teacher then reads the directions, which explain that this is a different kind of test than the tests the children usually take in school, because this test asks them to do all the different kinds of math problems they will learn this year in first grade. The directions further explain that the children's job is to complete all the problems they know how to do and skip the problems they do not know how to do. The children are told to work quickly but to make sure they work carefully. Then the teacher tells them to turn the test over and start working. At the end of 2 minutes, the teacher tells them to stop and collects the tests. The teacher does two practice tests with the class, on 2 consecutive days. On the third day, the teacher administers the real screening test. Each of the practice tests and the real test are alternative forms: Each alternative form has different problems but samples the same problem types in the

Practice List 1		
of	always	story
on	does	south
from	need	half
all	light	held
some	almost	table
them	kind	miles
him	better	that's
may	name	women
down	several	town
called	living	english
our	across	green
used	really	surface
come	means	coming
still	able	ask
life	book	books
between	inside	warm
few	anything	

FIGURE 2.1. Word Identification Fluency example list. Reprinted with permission from Lynn S. Fuchs.

same proportion, and problems are displayed in a different order on each of the three alternative forms.

CBM Concepts and Applications is a 25-item test sampling the typical first-grade concepts and applications curriculum (numeration, concepts, geometry, measurement, applied computation, money, charts/graphs, word problems). As with CBM Calculations, it is administered in whole-class format, with similar directions and two practice tests. However, in contrast to CBM Calculations, the teacher paces the class through the problems, reading the words in each problem aloud, problem by problem. For the first 20 problems, the teacher gives students 15 seconds to respond; for the last five problems, they have 30 seconds to respond. Students are designated as being at risk when their CBM Calculations score is less than 4, *and* their CBM Concepts and Applications score is less than 12. In many schools, scoring below the screening test's cut point provides the basis for secondary (Tier 2) intervention.

Sheet # 2

Password: All

Computation 1 – rev.

6 + 0 = _____	7 2 + 0	41 + 21	3 + 4 = _____	4 – 3 = _____
10 – 9 = _____	9 + 1 = _____	9 – 3 = _____	7 – 3 = _____	1 + 0 = _____
6 3 + 0	14 – 0	5 + 0 = _____	7 + 1 = _____	5 – 0 = _____
1 + 4 = _____	7 – 4 = _____	9 – 8 = _____	7 + 2 = _____	8 – 5 = _____
5 – 3 = _____	3 – 2 = _____	8 + 2 = _____	10 + 24	57 – 4

FIGURE 2.2. CBM Calculations example test. Reprinted with permission from Lynn S. Fuchs.

It is important to note that, as with all screening assessments, the designated cut point for Word Identification Fluency and for CBM Concepts and Applications is not perfect in distinguishing students who are and are not at risk. In fact, cut points are often purposefully set high enough to avoid missing any truly at-risk students. Thus, it is better to think of students identified via universal screening as *suspected* to be at risk. The students mistakenly identified as at risk are referred to as *false positives*. This is similar to how testing works in medicine. For example, many women are screened with mammograms, but mammograms produce many false positives. Rather than perform surgery on all women with suspicious mammograms, additional testing (e.g., sonograms or magnetic resonance imaging [MRI]) is conducted to greatly reduce the number of women who undergo surgery.

Back to screening in the context of tiered systems of support, false positives can be costly for three reasons. First, providing intervention is expensive. Second, falsely positive students (those who are misidentified as needing support) do not require intervention (they do fine without it), and they may in fact profit more from the general education program than from intervention, as suggested in a recent national evaluation of response to intervention (RTI) (Balu et al., 2015; Fuchs & Fuchs, 2017). Third, a large number of false positives can flood a school's intervention system and thereby dilute the quality of secondary (Tier 2) intervention available for students who do require that support.

For these reasons, we recommend that schools follow up universal screening (the brief tests administered to everyone in the school) with a second round of assessment, or *second-stage screening,* using a different, individually administered test for the subset of students who are suspected to be at risk via universal screening (D. Fuchs, Fuchs, & Compton, 2012). For example, the teacher might confirm or disconfirm risk by administering a different reading or math test, designed for more thorough assessment, such as the Wide Range Achievement Test—Reading or Math Calculations (Wilkinson & Robertson, 2006) (reading and/or math depending on whether the student's risk designation was in reading and/or math).

Alternatively, the teacher might monitor the progress—for 6–8 weeks—of the subset of students in the classroom suspected to be at risk. The resulting progress monitoring scores are used to confirm or disconfirm risk status. Only students who fail to demonstrate adequate progress over these 6–8 weeks move on to intervention.

PROGRESS MONITORING

With progress monitoring, students are assessed frequently, at least monthly, and the goal is to assess the *growth* of the student. The frequency of progress monitoring depends on how the progress monitoring data are to be used. In all cases, the scores are graphed against time, and a line of best fit is drawn through the graphed scores. For this line of best fit, a slope (estimating the weekly rate of increase) is calculated to quantify the student's rate of learning. Teachers can use progress monitoring slope, along with the student's current score, for three purposes: (1) to confirm or disconfirm suspected risk status (as just discussed), in which case data might be collected once every 2 weeks; (2) to determine whether a student is responding adequately to the Tier 2 instructional program (again, data are collected on alternating weeks); and (3) for students who prove unresponsive to a secondary (Tier 2) intervention, to inductively design individualized instructional plans (in this case, data should be collected weekly). With DBI, we use progress monitoring for this third purpose.

Two major forms of progress monitoring are mastery measurement and general outcome measurement. With mastery measurement, teachers assess mastery of a sequence of skills. Designing a mastery measurement progress monitoring system requires two major tasks. The first requires determining the hierarchy of skills for instruction. For example, with first-grade reading, one might specify the following sequence of skills: letter–sound correspondence, decoding phonemically regular consonant–vowel–consonant words, decoding phonemically regular consonant–vowel–consonant–final *e* words, automatically recognizing the 100 most frequent Dolch words, decoding pho-nemically regular *r*-controlled words, and so on. The second major task in creating a mastery measurement progress monitoring system is to design a criterion-referenced test for each skill in the instructional hierarchy. So, for example, for letter–sound cor-respondence, the criterion-referenced test might involve presenting students with a shuffled deck of letters, one letter at a time for 1 minute; the student responds by saying the sounds associated with the letters; the score is the number correct. The criterion for mastery might be 26 letter sounds in 1 minute on two consecutive tests. When the stu-dent achieves the mastery criterion, then instruction and testing simultaneously shift to the next skill in the hierarchy, decoding phonemically regular consonant–vowel–consonant words, for which a criterion-referenced test is also designed. Most classroom-based reading assessments fall into the category of mastery measurement.

Mastery measurement systems, however, often demonstrate technical problems, which can limit their utility for evaluating trends in progress over time. For example, achievement as indexed on the mastery measurement system (i.e., number of skills mas-tered across a school year) sometimes does not correspond well to performance at the end of the year on high-stakes tests. Poor correspondence, with some children who have mastered many skills performing surprisingly poorly on the high-stakes end-of-year testing, can occur due to poor retention of previously mastered skills. For example, a student might master consonant–vowel–consonant words, but when instruction and testing simultaneously shift to the next skill in the hierarchy, the student's accuracy in decoding consonant–vowel–consonant words deteriorates.

Another source of poor correspondence between the number of skills mastered and final performance on the high-stakes test is mastery measurement's reliance on a *single-skill* testing framework. Some students can perform a skill competently only because they know that every item on the test represents an example of the target skill. For example, some students decode consonant–vowel–consonant words accurately when all the words on the test represent that pattern; they know to incorporate the short vowel for every word on the test. Some subset of these students, however, cannot decode consonant–vowel–consonant words when consonant–vowel–consonant words are presented in mixed-skill fashion, along with words of a variety of phonetic cat-egories. In contrast to mastery measurement, high-stakes tests do not rely on single-skill measurement. Hence the potential exists for poor correspondence between per-formance on mastery measurement's single-skill testing framework versus high-stakes tests' sampling across many skills.

For these and other reasons, over the past 30 years, an alternative form of progress monitoring has been developed and has gained popularity. This alternative form of progress monitoring is known as *general outcome measurement*, which simultaneously assesses performance across the many skills represented in the annual curriculum. Research indicates that general outcome progress monitoring represents a technically superior framework for progress monitoring, relating better to end-of-year high-stakes test performance.

General outcome measurement differs from most forms of classroom assessment in three ways. First, general outcome measurement is standardized, so that the behaviors to be measured and the procedures for measuring those behaviors are prescribed. This ensures that the assessment scores are accurate. Second, the focus of general outcome measurement is long term, so that testing methods and content remain constant; that is, each weekly test is of equivalent difficulty and spans the entire school year. The primary reason for long-term consistency is so that teachers can compare scores in September to scores collected at any other time of year to determine whether the student has improved. Third, general outcome measurement is usually fluency based, so that students have a fixed amount of time to respond to the test. Therefore, improvement reflects an individual's capacity to perform critical behaviors with accuracy and ease.

CBM is the form of general outcome progress monitoring for which most of the research has been conducted. CBM has been shown to be more sensitive for detecting student improvement than the more common mastery measurement framework. In addition, CBM has been shown to reveal student improvement regardless of the instructional approach the teacher uses (explicit, balanced, constructivist). Also, with CBM, teachers incorporate a wide range of instructional methods. So CBM general outcome measurement and the progress monitoring model are not tied to any particular instructional approach. This permits teachers to experiment with curricula, intervention programs, instructional adaptations, and major program revisions in an attempt to improve learning, while maintaining the progress monitoring system constant. Research shows that when teachers use CBM progress monitoring to help them tailor their instruction to match students' instructional needs, it can have a positive effect on achievement among their students.

CBM can take one of two forms. It can systematically sample the curriculum or can rely on a single behavior that functions as an overall indicator of competence in an academic area. In mathematics, the dominant strategy for general outcome measurement is based on curriculum sampling, in which the problem types taught across the school year are identified; each problem type's emphasis in the curriculum is designated, and item banks for each problem type are created. Alternative CBM test forms are generated by sampling items from the item banks in the correct proportion, so that each alternative form represents the annual curriculum in the same ways. Problems are presented in random order on each test. In math, the most common probes rely on the curriculum sampling approach that systematically samples the variety of problem types represented in that grade's state standards.

In reading, most CBM systems rely on the overall indicator approach. Table 2.1 identifies the most common CBM measures in reading for elementary and middle school grades. A more detailed description of reading CBM, with examples, follows.

At kindergarten, the major alternatives for CBM reading measures are *phoneme segmentation fluency, rapid letter naming, and letter–sound fluency.* With phoneme segmentation fluency, the examiner says a word; the student says its constituent sounds. The examiner presents as many words within 1 minute as the rate of the child's response permits. With rapid letter naming, the examiner presents a page of lower- and uppercase letters randomly ordered; the student says as many letter names as he or she can in 1 minute. With letter–sound fluency, the examiner also presents a page with lower- and uppercase letters randomly ordered; this time, however, the student says sounds for 1 minute. Compared to phoneme segmentation fluency, rapid letter naming and letter–sound fluency are easier for teachers to learn to administer, and reliability tends to be

TABLE 2.1. Common CBM Measures in Reading for Elementary and Middle School Grades

	K	1	2	3	4	5	6	7	8
Letter Naming Fluency	x	x							
Letter–Sound Fluency	x	x							
Phonemic Segmentation	x	x							
Nonsense Word Fluency	x	x							
Word Identification Fluency	x	x							
Oral Reading Fluency		x	x	x	x	x	x	x	x
Passage Reading Fluency			x	x	x	x			
Cloze					x	x	x	x	x
Maze (multiple-choice cloze task)					x	x	x	x	x

Note. Suggested grade levels reflect typical skills development. For students with disabilities or those at risk who perform below grade-level standards, progress monitoring should occur at the instructional level.

stronger. On the other hand, compared to rapid letter naming, phoneme segmentation fluency and letter–sound fluency are better targets for instruction, because they relate more transparently to what children need for learning to read. For this reason, it is possible that phoneme segmentation fluency and letter–sound fluency will guide the kindergarten teacher's instructional behavior more effectively.

At first grade, two CBM reading measures have been studied and have evidence of technical adequacy. One approach involves combining *nonsense word fluency* and *passage reading fluency* (sometimes called *oral reading fluency*): Students begin the year on nonsense word fluency and move to the more difficult performance indicator, passage reading fluency, in January. With nonsense word fluency, students are presented with a page of consonant–vowel–consonant (with some vowel–consonant) pseudowords and have 1 minute to decode as many as they can. With passage reading fluency, the teacher presents the student with an instructional-level passage (each test is an alternative form of roughly comparable difficulty). The student reads aloud for 1 minute; the score is the number of words read correctly. Alternatively, schools use a constant measure across all of first grade: *word identification fluency*, as described earlier in this chapter in the section on screening.

The advantage of nonsense word fluency is that it maps onto beginning decoding instruction, potentially providing teachers with specific information about errors to inform instructional planning. The downside of the nonsense word fluency/passage reading fluency combination is that getting a meaningful picture of development over the full course of first grade is problematic—teachers cannot compare scores collected in the first half of the year with scores collected after passage reading fluency begins. By contrast, word identification fluency can be used with strong reliability, validity, and instructional usefulness across the entire first-grade year (L. S. Fuchs et al., 2004). This also makes it possible to get a good picture of a student's reading development across the entire time frame.

At grades 2 and 3, the CBM passage reading fluency measure provides the strongest source of information on reading development. The reliability, validity, and instructional utility of this simple measure have been demonstrated repeatedly. Some teachers can think of students whose comprehension is weak despite good fluency. It is important to note that these students are memorable because they are few and far between. In the vast majority of cases, students who have strong fluency are the same students who also demonstrate good comprehension.

Some research indicates that the validity of the CBM passage reading fluency task decreases beginning at grade 4 or grade 5. So, at these grades, teachers should consider using a different measure that more directly taps comprehension. Two alternatives for the higher elementary grades are *cloze* and *maze fluency*. In the cloze procedure, words are omitted from a passage, and students are required to fill in the blanks. Maze fluency is similar to cloze, in that students are presented with a passage from which words have been deleted; however, with maze fluency, the omitted words are replaced with three possible words, only one of which is semantically tenable. The student has 2.5 minutes to read and replace blanks, and the score is the number of correct replacements (with three consecutive errors used as a ceiling). Some research indicates that maze fluency demonstrates strong reliability and validity, and models reading development beginning at grade 4 and continuing through eighth grade. See Table 2.2 for example cloze and maze items.

DIAGNOSTIC ASSESSMENT

In this chapter, we define "diagnosis" to mean assessment that describes a student's strengths and weaknesses on skills or strategies (we do *not* use this term to denote diagnosing a student's disability). Diagnostic assessment is typically conducted periodically, when a teacher is concerned about a student's lack of progress, to identify the skills on which the student is strong and weak. Within DBI, diagnostic assessment is the third of the five steps described by Peterson et al. (Chapter 1, this volume). The goal is to identify productive targets for instruction. Hence, if a diagnostic assessment instrument indicates that the student is strong in decoding but lacks fluency, the teacher would direct his or her instruction toward fluency. If a diagnostic assessment instrument indicates that the student decodes *r*-controlled words accurately but cannot decode two-syllable words with an open first syllable, the teacher would direct his or her instruction toward this type of two-syllable word.

TABLE 2.2. Cloze and Maze Examples

Question type	Example
Cloze	Maria loves to _____ piano.
Maze	Maria loves to [plan—play—put] piano. She [positive—practices—promises] every day. She wants to be a [professional—promising—protect] musician someday.

We provide an example of a diagnostic tool that addresses the skills pertinent to developing readers. It is designed to be used in conjunction with CBM passage reading fluency (as already discussed), with which teachers analyze CBM graphs to determine when a student's rate of improvement is adequate. Inadequate progress signals the teacher to adjust the student's instructional program in a way designed to produce a better rate of improvement.

The diagnostic system we describe extends this CBM framework in two ways. First, CBM passage reading fluency cut scores are provided to determine whether a student's instructional change should focus on decoding, fluency, or comprehension. If the student's CBM score falls below a given cut score for that grade level, then the recommendation is for the teacher to focus the intervention adjustment on decoding instruction for that student; if the student's CBM score is above the cut score for that grade level, then the recommendation is for the teacher to focus on fluency building; if the student's CBM score exceeds a second (higher) cut score, then the recommendation is for the teacher to focus the intervention adjustment on comprehension.

Second, for students who require decoding instruction, a brief follow-up assessment is also conducted to determine which decoding skills the student has and has not mastered. This diagnostic assessment includes 48 pseudowords, representing seven phonetic categories (six words per category); words are ordered in terms of difficulty (not necessarily by categories). The assessment is administered with basals and ceilings to minimize frustration and test time. Based on the number of words read correctly in each category, mastery/nonmastery is designated for each category.

Figure 2.3 shows a CBM graph representing Shaun's progress toward becoming a competent reader in second-grade material. Below the graph, the decoding skills diagnostic profile is shown. Each row represents performance on one of the seven decoding skills; the horizontal axis of the graph designates time for the skills profile, so that the first column of boxes describes performance during October. Accordingly, each box describes performance on one phonetic category at one point in time. Keys explain the patterns in the boxes (with increasing darkness representing greater mastery) and the names of the decoding skills with examples of real words that illustrate the patterns. For example, as shown in Figure 2.3, Shaun's performance on MAT/LAST (consonant–vowel–consonant; consonant–vowel–consonant–consonant) words improved from October to December, and at present, in December, he is decoding most MAT/LAST and CAR (r-controlled) words. However, he is still struggling with PUBLIC (unlike consonants). This illustrates how diagnostic assessment can be used in conjunction with progress monitoring data in the DBI process.

CONSIDERATIONS FOR IMPLEMENTING ASSESSMENT WITHIN DBI

Now that we have described the three different purposes of assessment within DBI, we turn to some important considerations for implementation, including how to select a screening or progress monitoring tool, how to analyze progress monitoring data, and issues related to the secondary school context.

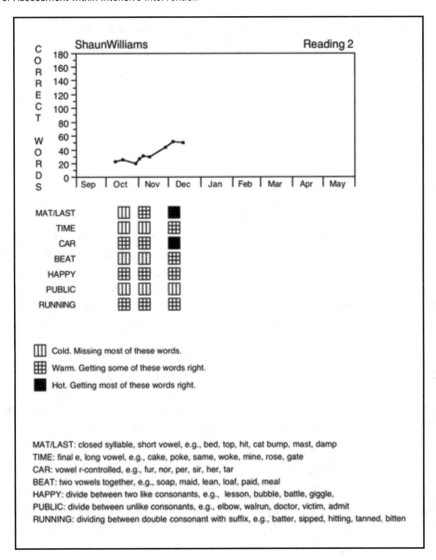

FIGURE 2.3. CBM graph.

Selecting a Screening or Progress Monitoring Tool

When identifying screening and progress monitoring tools, it is often challenging to distinguish what makes one tool better than another. To address this challenge, the National Center on Intensive Intervention (NCII) developed four tools charts that are available to assist educators and families in becoming informed consumers who can select academic and behavioral screening and progress monitoring tools, as well as interventions that best meet individual student needs (*www.intensiveintervention.org/ resources/tools-charts*). These tools charts display expert ratings on the technical rigor of screening and progress monitoring assessments. The reviews are conducted by an external Technical Review Committee of experts, and assessment tools are rated against established criteria and not ranked or compared to each other. When selecting a tool, it is important to consider both the technical rigor of the tool and your needs and priorities. (Note that not all available screening and progress monitoring tools are listed on the chart—only tools that have been submitted by the tool vendor appear on the chart.)

Using the NCII Tools Charts

For each tools chart, the review content is grouped in three "tabs" or sets of standards across the top of each chart. For the Academic and Behavior Screening charts, the three tabs are *classification accuracy, technical standards, and usability features*. For the Academic and Behavior Progress Monitoring charts, the three tabs are *foundational psychometric standards, progress monitoring with intensive populations,* and *usability features*. Users can click on one of these tabs to see that *set* of standards (see Figure 2.4). The bubbles on the tools chart are indicators of the technical rigor of the tools and may be filled completely, partially, or not at all. Clicking on the *title* of each standard at the top of the column will bring up information on the standard and what the bubble ratings mean for that standard. Clicking on an evidence *bubble* for a tool will bring up the supporting information for the tool's rating on that standard. Note that the screening charts provide ratings by grade, and the progress monitoring charts provide ratings by grade and subscale.

Additional information on using the Tools Charts can be found in Tools Charts Users Guide (*www.intensiveintervention.org/tools-chart-resources*). In that guide the NCII

Tab 1: Classification Accuracy

Criterion 1 Fall	Criterion 1 Winter	Criterion 1 Spring	Criterion 2 Fall	Criterion 2 Winter	Criterion 2 Spring
●d	●	●	○	◐	○

d = disaggregated data available

Tab 2: Technical Standards

Reliability	Validity	Sample Representativeness	Bias Analysis Conducted
●	●	●	Yes/No

Tab 3: Usability Features

Administration Format	Administration and Scoring Time	Scoring Format	Types of Decision Rules	Evidence Available for Multiple Decision Rules
Group/ Individual	# minutes	Automatic/ Manual	Moderate/ Intensive/None	Yes/No

FIGURE 2.4. NCII Progress Monitoring Tools Chart tabs.

notes that the "best" tool is not the same for all schools or for all students in that school. NCII encourages users to review all the elements of the chart before making decisions and recommends the following six steps as consumers make decisions:

1. Gather a team.
2. Determine your needs.
3. Determine your priorities.
4. Familiarize yourself with the content and language of the chart.
5. Review the data.
6. Ask for more information.

APPLICATION EXERCISE 2.1. Identifying High-Quality Screening or Progress Monitoring Tools Using the NCII Tools Charts

Set the NCII Screening Tools Chart to show mathematics tools for first grade and identify the following:

1. Find a screening tool offering assessment of early numeracy.
2. Identify a screening tool that has convincing evidence for classification accuracy (e.g., the tool accurately classifies students into "at risk for math disability" and "not at risk for math disability" categories).

Set the NCII Academic Progress Monitoring chart to show reading tools for second grade and identify the following:

1. Find at least two progress monitoring tools offering the maze reading assessment.
2. Identify an Oral Reading Fluency tool that has convincing evidence of reliability and validity.

Analyzing Progress Monitoring Data to Make Decisions

As previously established, progress monitoring data help us decide when instructional changes need to be made. If a student is not responding sufficiently to the standard secondary (Tier 2) platform, the intensive intervention process should begin. In turn, if the student's response to the intensive intervention platform is not adequate, additional adaptations to the platform should occur. Analyzing graphed progress monitoring data will help you determine whether a student is responsive, which will tell you whether to continue with the current intervention or make a change.

The question teachers frequently grapple with when graphing progress monitoring data is: How much progress monitoring data are necessary to make a sound decision? Recommendations include six to nine data points (Christ & Silberglitt, 2007), with more frequent progress monitoring allowing for instructional decisions to be made sooner. There are two methods for systematically making decisions about instructional changes: (1) the 4-point rule and (2) trendline analysis.

Using the 4-Point Rule

After six progress monitoring data points have been collected and graphed, examine the four most recent data points and use the following guidelines:

- If all four are above the goal line, increase the goal.
- If all four are below the goal line, make an instructional change.
- If the four data points are both above and below the goal line, keep collecting data until the 4-point rule can be applied (or consider trend analysis—explained in the next exercise).
- If you reach 9 data points, without 4 consecutive points all above or below the goal line, then draw a line of best fit through the most recent 9 data points. If the line of best fit is steeper than the goal line, raise the goal. If the line of best fit is less steep than the goal line, make an adaptation to the platform.

Using the Combined 4-Point Rule
and Trendline Analysis

After six progress monitoring data points have been collected and graphed, examine the four most recent data points and use the following guidelines:

- Calculate the trend of current performance (by hand or with software). Note that trendlines are often calculated using software. For drawing trendlines by hand, please see the RTI Implementer Series Module 2: Progress Monitoring (National Center on Response to Intervention, 2012).
- Compare to the goal line.
- If the student's trendline is steeper than the goal line, increase the goal.
- If the student's trendline is flatter than the goal line, make a change to the intervention.
- If the student's trendline and the goal line are the same, no changes need to be made.

APPLICATION EXERCISE 2.2. Analyzing Data to Make Decisions

Practice with the 4-Point Rule

- Examine the graphed progress monitoring data for students Alycia and Mandy in Figures 2.5 and 2.6, respectively, and determine next steps based upon the 4-point rule guidelines.
- *Answer for Alycia:* Alycia's four most recent scores are below the goal line. Therefore, the teacher needs to change her instructional program. The end-of-year performance goal and goal line never decrease; they can increase only. The instructional program should be tailored to bring Alycia's scores up so they match or surpass the goal line (Figure 2.5).
- *Answer for Mandy:* All of Mandy's most recent four data points were above the goal line.

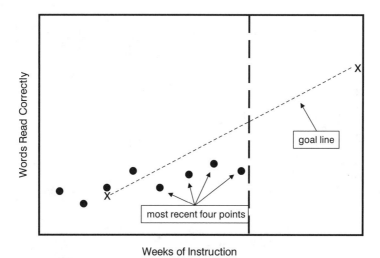

FIGURE 2.5. Four-point rule graph for Alycia.

This suggests that her teacher should increase her goal. If she reaches the grade-level benchmark, her teacher may consider reducing the intensity of her supports (Figure 2.6).

- *Note on the advantages/disadvantages of the four-point rule:* The advantage of the 4-point rule is that it is easy to conduct given that it does not require calculating a trendline. The disadvantage is that it is not very sensitive. An outlier score could delay making a decision by preventing four consecutive scores falling above or below the goal line. In these types of situations, it is best to combine both the 4-point rule and the trendline analysis (as illustrated).

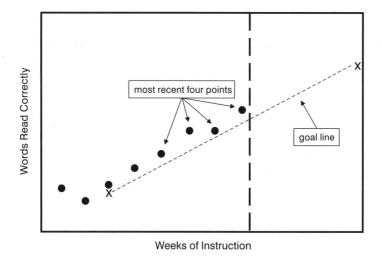

FIGURE 2.6. Four-point rule graph for Mandy.

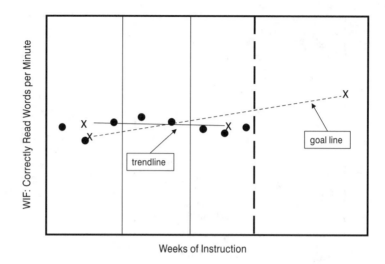

FIGURE 2.7. Four-point rule and trendline analysis graph for Jared.

Practice with the Combined 4-Point Rule and Trendline Analysis

- Examine the graphs below. Based on the goal and trendlines, what instructional decisions would you make for each student?
- *Answer for Jared:* Jared's four most recent points are not all below the goal line; however, the trendline is below and flatter than the goal line, so an instructional change is needed (Figure 2.7).
- *Answer for Mario:* Mario's trend line is above the goal line. This suggests that his teacher should increase his goal. If he reaches the grade-level benchmark, his teacher may consider reducing the intensity of his supports (Figure 2.8).

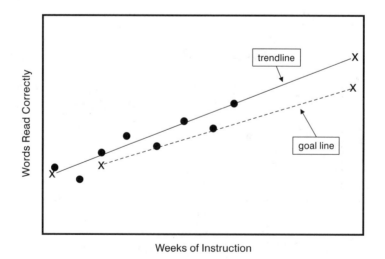

FIGURE 2.8. Four-point rule and trendline analysis graph for Mario.

Considerations at Middle and High School

Implementing the DBI process (to include essential assessment components) at middle and high school presents a unique set of challenges in comparison to those seen in an elementary school setting. These challenges occur at both the school level (e.g., roles and responsibilities of staff members, schedules and structures, graduation requirements) and the student level (e.g., more severe reading or math deficits and motivation issues). Although the majority of research around tiered systems of support has been conducted at elementary grade levels (Brozo, 2010), some research groups provide instructive guidance about implementing intensive intervention and using effective methods of assessment at middle and high school (e.g., Pyle & Vaughn, 2012; Vaughn & Fletcher, 2012).

With regard to screening, given that the academic deficits of students in middle and high school are often well established, it is often easier to identify students at risk for academic failure in middle and high school than in an elementary setting. Therefore, schools may consider relying on teacher nominations or existing assessment data (e.g., state reading assessment) to identify students at risk, as opposed to allocating resources to universal screening processes as is usually necessary in elementary settings (L. S. Fuchs, Fuchs, & Compton, 2010). An important caveat to use of a state measure for screening purposes is the need to carefully examine the validity and reliability of the measure, as well as technical basis for the cut point and standard error. Additionally, when examining the results of these assessments, practitioners at middle and high school may want to consider placing severely discrepant students immediately in the most intensive level of a tiered system of support (i.e., Tier 3) to ensure that students with sizable deficits receive the level of support required.

For progress monitoring, research conducted at middle and high school indicates that it may be possible to measure the progress of secondary students less frequently than elementary students (who are often administered progress monitoring assessments weekly or biweekly). Specifically, fluency may be measured with older students less frequently, because their reading performance grows more slowly over the year. Additionally, older students' reading growth typically plateaus in the later years, so it may be more effective to assess students' skills with proximal measures to monitor responsiveness to tasks taught in a content area (Barth et al., 2012; Espin, Wallace, Lembke, Campbell, & Long, 2010).

Finally, diagnostic assessment should continue to play an important role in secondary settings in identifying students' strengths and weaknesses in skills. As in elementary settings, gathering additional diagnostic information can help to identify productive targets for instruction. For example, adding a diagnostic assessment, such as an oral reading fluency measure, to a reading comprehension assessment can provide significant diagnostic information about secondary students with reading difficulties, without requiring substantial teacher time (Vaughn & Fletcher, 2012).

SUMMARY

Guidance provided in this chapter can support teachers as they use assessment tools to make data-based decisions in a tiered system of supports that includes intensive intervention. Effective use of screening, progress monitoring and, diagnostic assessment is an essential component of the DBI process and drives successful data-based decision making. Within the context of DBI, the use of high-quality assessment tools helps practitioners confidently identify students who are in need of intensive intervention, understand which skills are high priority for instructional focus, and identify not only when instructional changes are required but also what may be a productive direction for those instructional changes. This use of assessment is the foundation for the process of individualizing and intensifying interventions and drives teachers' decision making in DBI.

FREQUENTLY ASKED QUESTIONS

How can assessment help you communicate with parents/families about their children's needs?

Data on a child's progress is perhaps the most effective tool at a teacher's disposal for communicating with a family about the child's instructional needs, goals, and program. Screening data can help school staff members determine the need for intervention, and diagnostic data can offer useful information to guide a conversation with families about what kinds of interventions and instructional strategies might be needed. Graphed progress monitoring data allow family members and school staff members together to regularly review the student's progress and response to changes in instruction. By focusing their conversations on data, families and schools can work in partnership toward shared goals that are informed by objective evidence. And, when students make progress, the data can be used to celebrate success!

How is screening related to intensive intervention?

Screening is the first step to identifying students who may be at risk of academic failure and who require intervention instruction, in addition to core instruction. Within the context of DBI, screening is not typically used to identify students in need of intensive intervention; however, it is an essential component of a tiered support system and critical for understanding risk levels. Note that there are some cases in which screening data might indicate that a student should move immediately into intensive intervention rather than moving through each level of support embedded within an MTSS framework.

When should diagnostic assessment be used?

Diagnostic assessment in intensive intervention is intended to be informal and brief; it may include error analysis, skills analysis, or other reviews of relevant data; and it is used to reveal information about student's strengths and weaknesses on skills or strategies. Results from diagnostic assessment should directly inform intensive intervention as teachers work to adapt instruction to meet these individualized needs. Therefore, diagnostic assessment is conducted periodically when a teacher is concerned about a student's lack of progress, to identify the skills on which the student is strong and weak.

Is weekly data collection necessary for implementing DBI or is less frequent (intermittent) data collection adequate?

For DBI, weekly academic progress monitoring is recommended, because frequent decision making is critical for optimizing the learning outcomes of intensive intervention students, and weekly data collection supports more frequent decision making than does intermittent data collection. This is the case for two reasons. First, with intermittent data collection (every 2–3 or 4–6 weeks), no decisions are possible in the intervening (nonmeasurement) weeks. Second, intermittent data collection does not permit the use of optimal DBI decision rules, in which teachers make program changes when the trendline (slope of improvement) is less steep than the goal line *or* when four consecutive data points fall below the goal line. With intermittent data collection, the consecutive data points part of this rule requires too much time to pass (e.g., a 3-week data collection schedule requires 3 months to generate a decision; a 4-week data collection schedule requires 4 months). Therefore, intermittent data collection provides a weaker data source for making timely DBI decisions. To produce timely DBI decision rules, we recommend that teachers collect progress monitoring weekly and use the decision rule that combines the trendline decision with the 4-consecutive-point decision.

When implementing DBI, can I use below-grade-level material to monitor progress and can I remediate foundational (below-grade-level) skills?

Yes and yes. Monitoring progress at the instructional level has been shown to provide a more adequate basis for indexing student improvement. Remediating foundational (below-grade-level) skills has been shown to be important for realizing improvement on grade-level content. Whenever possible, teachers should remediate skills in conjunction with instruction that also addresses grade-level content.

REFERENCES

Al Otaiba, S., Wagner, R. K., & Miller, B. (2014). "Waiting to fail" redux: Understanding inadequate response to intervention. *Learning Disability Quarterly, 37*(3), 129–133.

Balu, R., Zhu, P., Doolittle, F., Schiller, E., Jenkins, J., & Gersten, R. (2015). *Evaluation of response to intervention practices for elementary school reading* (NCEE 2016-4000). Washington, DC: National Center for Education Evaluation and Regional Assistance.

Barth, A. E., Stuebing, K. K., Fletcher, J. M., Cirino, P. T., Francis, D. J., & Vaughn, S. (2012). Reliability and validity of the median score when assessing the oral reading fluency of middle grade readers. *Reading Psychology, 33*(1–2), 133–161.

Brozo, W. G. (2010). The role of content literacy in an effective RTI program. *The Reading Teacher, 64*(2), 147–150.

Christ, T. J., & Silberglitt, B. (2007). Estimates of the standard error of measurement for curriculum-based measures of oral reading fluency. *School Psychology Review, 36*(1), 130.

Espin, C., Wallace, T., Lembke, E., Campbell, H., & Long, J. D. (2010). Creating a progress-monitoring system in reading for middle-school students: Tracking progress toward meeting high-stakes standards. *Learning Disabilities Research and Practice, 25*(2), 60–75.

Fuchs, D., & Fuchs, L. S. (2017). Critique of the National Evaluation of Response to Intervention: A case for simpler frameworks. *Exceptional Children, 83*(3), 255–268.

Fuchs, D., Fuchs, L. S., & Compton, D. L. (2012). Smart RTI: A next-generation approach to multi-level prevention. *Exceptional Children, 78*(3), 263–279.

Fuchs, L. S., Fuchs, D., & Compton, D. L. (2004). Monitoring early reading development in first grade: Word identification fluency versus nonsense word fluency. *Exceptional Children, 71*(1), 7–21.

Fuchs, L. S., Fuchs, D., & Compton, D. L. (2010). Rethinking response to intervention at middle and high school. *School Psychology Review, 39*(1), 22–28.

Fuchs, L. S., Hamlett, C., & Fuchs, D. (1990). *Monitoring basic skills progress* [Computer program]. Austin, TX: PRO-ED.

National Center on Response to Intervention. (2012). *RTI implementer series: Module 2. Progress monitoring.* Washington, DC: U.S. Department of Education, Office of Special Education Programs, National Center on Response to Intervention.

Pyle, N., & Vaughn, S. (2012). Remediating reading difficulties in a response to intervention model with secondary students. *Psychology in the Schools, 49*(3), 273–284.

Vaughn, S., & Fletcher, J. M. (2012). Response to intervention with secondary school students with reading difficulties. *Journal of Learning Disabilities, 45*(3), 244–256.

Wilkinson, G., & Robertson, G. (2006). *Wide Range Achievement Test 4: Professional manual.* Lutz, FL: Psychological Assessment Resources.

CHAPTER 3

Integrating Behavior and Academics in Intervention Planning

LAURA BERRY KUCHLE
T. CHRIS RILEY-TILLMAN

GUIDING QUESTIONS

➤ Why is it important to address both academic and behavioral needs in an integrated intensive intervention plan?

➤ How is data-based individualization for behavior and academics combined similar to and different from data-based individualization for academics alone?

➤ How do I start planning an intervention for a student who has both academic and behavioral needs?

As described by Peterson, Danielson, and Fuchs (Chapter 1, this volume), data-based individualization (DBI) is a systematic process for using student-level data to determine when and how to adapt intensive intervention (National Center on Intensive Intervention [NCII], 2013a). While this book focuses primarily on providing intensive intervention in academics, students with the most intensive needs often have interrelated challenges in both academics and behavior, requiring integrated planning and supports (Berry Kuchle, Zumeta Edmonds, Danielson, Peterson, & Riley-Tillman, 2015). For example, students with severe behavior problems may need academic supports to provide instruction they missed as a result of extreme behavior problems, and students with learning disabilities may need behavioral or motivational supports to help them engage in tasks that have historically been difficult and frustrating. In both groups, mechanisms for supporting their "on-task" behavior and addressing issues related to attention problems also may be beneficial. If inadequately addressed, emotional or behavioral concerns can reduce academic engagement and achievement and lead to more significant long-term behavior issues (Burns, Riley-Tillman, & VanDerHayden,

2012). Youth diagnosed with an emotional disturbance have the highest arrest rates of any disability group (49.4% compared to 12% for the general population; Sanford et al., 2011) and the highest high school dropout rates (35%) of any disability category (McFarland et al., 2017). Similarly, academic struggles may be predictive of some behavior concerns. For example, young adults with learning disabilities have arrest rates much higher than the general population (22.3 and 12%, respectively; Sanford et al., 2011). Taken together, these data suggest that when children exhibit both academic and behavioral problems, we should address both areas fully.

We discuss in this chapter how to plan, implement, and monitor integrated academic and behavioral intervention using a similar approach to that described in the rest of the book for academics. The goal of addressing both areas simultaneously is to provide more effective and more individualized intensive intervention. Figure 3.1 provides examples of how the DBI process may look in each area and for an integrated plan. The steps are conceptually similar regardless of area, although there are some differences when applying DBI to behavior compared to academics, as seen in Table 3.1.

In an integrated intensive intervention plan, we start with evidence-based interventions or strategies that address the student's needs, both academic and behavioral. We progress monitor in both academics and behavior to determine whether the initial intervention is effective for both areas of need. If the child does not respond sufficiently, we engage in diagnostic assessment, typically referred to as "functional assessment for behavior." Functional assessment, described later in this chapter, helps educators identify why the problem behavior is occurring (our hypothesis) and guides the selection and adaptation (when needed) of an evidence-based intervention to help the child. For integrated plans, it is important to consider both academic and behavioral hypotheses, paying particular attention to how behavioral and academic needs interact with one another. Ongoing progress monitoring allows educators to evaluate the child's response to the new or adapted intervention, making further changes to academic and/or behavioral supports as needed. It is important to note that a student requiring intensive intervention may have intensive needs in both academics and behavior, or may have intensive needs only in one area while requiring a lesser degree of support in the other. We use the DBI process to integrate supports in both areas regardless of intensity, as long as needs are intensive in at least one area.

Although we focus more on behavior intervention selection and progress monitoring throughout this chapter, this does not suggest that academic and behavior intervention should be conducted in isolation. We advocate for integrated supports but focus on behavior here, because other chapters focus on academic assessment and intensive intervention.

WHERE DO I START?

While it might be simpler if every intervention case were solely academic or behavioral, anyone who spends time in schools knows that children who have intensive needs often end up with both academic and social behavior needs. One of the first questions you should ask is whether you know the student's core or primary disability or problem. For

DBI Process	Academics	Behavior	Integrated
Validated Intervention Program (e.g., Tier 2, Standard Protocol, Secondary Intervention)	Evidence-based intervention that addresses the student's academic deficits	Evidence-based intervention or strategy that addresses the general category of the student's behavior	Combine evidence-based strategies that address the student's behavioral *and* academic needs
Progress Monitor	Technically rigorous tool at an appropriate level to capture the student's growth in skills targeted by the intervention and overall academic outcomes (e.g., curriculum-based measurement)	Technically rigorous tool or data collection method that is sensitive to change in the student's target behavior (e.g., direct observation, Direct Behavior Ratings)	Progress monitor *both* areas to make decisions about the academic and behavioral components of the integrated intervention
Diagnostic Data	Assessment used to identify a student's specific strengths and weaknesses within the academic area(s) of concern	Assessment to determine the function a behavior serves for the student (why is the student engaging in problem behavior or not performing expected behaviors?)	Form hypotheses for both academic *and* behavioral needs, with particular attention to how they interact
Intervention Adaptation	Adapt the intervention to address specific skill deficits, based on the hypothesis generated by diagnostic assessment	Adapt the intervention to better address the factors underlying behavior, based on the hypothesis generated by functional assessment	Adapt the intervention to simultaneously address both academic *and* behavioral needs based on diagnostic and functional assessment
Progress Monitor	Continue progress monitoring to determine when further intervention changes are needed, adjusting progress monitoring as needed to capture growth in targeted skills	Continue progress monitoring to determine when further intervention changes are needed, adjusting progress monitoring as needed to measure change in targeted behaviors	Continue progress monitoring in *both* areas so that intervention decisions are based on performance in both academics and behavior

FIGURE 3.1. NCII DBI process graphic with examples for academic, behavior, and integrated intensive intervention. Graphic reprinted with permission from the National Center on Intensive Intervention at the American Institutes for Research.

TABLE 3.1. Similarities and Differences in DBI for Academics and Behavior

Component	Similarities	Differences for behavior
Validated intervention program	Evidence-based for similar students with similar needs	• Fewer validated programs available; may rely more on evidence-based strategies rather than packaged programs
Progress monitoring	Valid, reliable tools that are sensitive to change for a given student	• Fewer validated tools available for behavior • May customize for specific student behaviors rather than measuring general outcomes • Fewer norms available for goal setting (more likely to base on individual history, peer norms, or school expectations) • Sometimes our goal is to decrease problem behavior (so we seek a downward trend in graphed data compared to the usual increasing trend for academics) • May see behavioral changes more quickly, especially if student can already perform expected behaviors • May need to monitor in multiple settings • Data may be more variable, requiring longer baseline

Diagnostic data	Assessment to generate hypotheses about *why* a student is struggling	• Focus on determining the function of behavior, which may include:
		  ○ Inability to perform desired behavior (social behavioral skills deficits)
		  ○ Failure to reinforce or generalize desired behavior
		  ○ Factors that maintain problem behavior

Intervention adaptation	Individualization to address hypotheses	• Based on function(s) of behavior • May need to teach or practice desired behavior and change conditions that maintain problem behavior

example, if a student with attention-deficit/hyperactivity disorder (ADHD) is behind in math because he or she struggles with attention and work completion, behavior/attention is the primary area of difficulty. The primary focus of intervention will be behavioral, to increase on-task behavior, with integrated math intervention until he or she catches up. *It is critical to note that you will still intervene in both areas of need, but the primary area may require more intensive support and monitoring, and may impact decisions you may make in other areas of concern.*

As noted earlier, students do not need to have intensive needs in both areas to benefit from integrated academic and behavioral intervention planning. Early integrated supports may allow you to address the secondary problem more easily, with less intensive supports. For example, a student with attention difficulties may initially achieve at grade level but slowly fall behind due to poor attention to instruction or missed practice opportunities (e.g., poor participation in class activities or homework). When we know a student has attentional or other behavioral difficulties, we should monitor academic performance so that we can (1) strengthen behavioral supports when needed to prevent further impact on academic performance and (2) remediate any academic difficulties as quickly as possible. It is easier for a student to catch up when he or she is only slightly behind academically rather than wait until he or she falls behind on screening or, worse, tests below grade level on annual achievement tests. Similarly, if a student with academic difficulties is not responding to academic intervention, we should consider behavioral explanations even if the student does not have obvious or intensive behavioral concerns. Is the student attentive to instruction, engaged in intervention, and motivated to perform his or her best during assessment? An integrated plan with a behavioral or motivational component may be more effective than academic intervention alone.

Although it is ideal to intervene early, when problems are less intense and perhaps only behavioral or academic in nature, in some cases, by the time you start working with a student, needs are intensive and long-standing in both areas. Under these circumstances, planning and hypothesis generation should simultaneously assess and address both academic needs and the function of behavior, with special attention to how academic and behavioral needs interact. For example, when a child exhibits intense escape behavior when presented with academic task demands (described in more detail in the section "Diagnostic Assessment and 'Function'"), we commonly find that he or she has significant weakness in those academic areas. In such a case, it is critical to utilize both academic and behavioral interventions concurrently to address the academic skills deficit and the problem behaviors maintained by escape. Ignoring either side of the equation will greatly minimize the likelihood of long-term success.

The next section focuses on identifying the function of behavior. Once you know the underlying academic and behavioral needs to address, you can select strategies that have been shown to address those needs for students similar to the target student. The NCII Behavioral Intervention Tools Chart (*https://intensiveintervention.org/chart/behavioral-intervention-chart*) is one resource to help identify evidence-based behavioral strategies. Appendix 3.1 lists additional resources to support intensive behavioral intervention planning.

The following application exercise introduces Jeremy, a student with both academic and behavioral concerns, and asks you to apply what you have learned in this section.

APPLICATION EXERCISE 3.1

Jeremy, a sixth-grade student with autism, has an above-average IQ and historically has been at or above grade level in all subjects, so his individualized education program (IEP) focuses on building social skills and establishing consistent routines to make him more comfortable in school. This year, however, he shows decreased academic engagement and sometimes refuses to do his work, especially in science class, where he is starting to fall behind academically.

Challenge: Can you identify Jeremy's core problem? How will this inform his integrated plan?

Discussion: Jeremy's primary problem historically has been behavioral. He did well academically in the past, and his current academic struggles seem to be tied to behaviors that interfere with learning (i.e., poor engagement, work refusal). It seems that in this case, behavior is the core focus and academic intervention, while important, is a secondary concern. His integrated supports will focus on a comprehensive behavioral plan, aimed at increasing academic engagement, with supports tailored to each school environment. He also will need academic remediation to help him catch up in science.

DIAGNOSTIC ASSESSMENT AND "FUNCTION"

Pentimonti, Fuchs, and Gandhi (Chapter 2, this volume) discussed academic diagnostic assessment in order to identify a student's specific needs; these needs guide academic intervention selection and adaptation. To select the most logical evidence-based behavioral intervention, we advocate starting with a functional approach to gain an understanding of why a child is exhibiting problem behavior. This is particularly important when there are co-occurring behavioral and academic needs, because needs in one area may be causing or maintaining problems in the other area. We may not be able to understand the function of some behaviors without considering academics.

A functional approach starts by considering what is happening in the classroom environment (or wherever the problem behavior occurs) that supports the problem behavior, and what changes could be made to increase the likelihood of a more desired behavioral outcome. This approach is often referred to as considering the "ABCs" of behavior.

- A for "antecedent"—the events that occur before the behavior.
- B for "behavior"—whatever it is that the child is doing that resulted in the concern. Note that the behavior must be measurable.
- C for "consequence"—the events that occur right after the behavior.

We are particularly interested in antecedents and consequences to understand what prompted the behavior (antecedents) and what is supporting the behavior (consequence). The goal of this approach is to hypothesize why the problem behavior makes sense given what the child receives and/or avoids as a result of the behavior; we also must determine whether the child has the skill to perform a desired alternative behavior that produces the same result. Generally speaking, this approach results in behaviors being categorized into four "functions."

1. *Positive reinforcement.* The problem behavior results in some desired outcome. For example, if the child desires teacher or peer attention, and problem behavior results in peers and the teacher focusing attention on the child, we hypothesize that the function of the behavior is attention seeking.

2. *Escape.* The problem behavior allows the child to avoid some outcome. Think about a child who cannot do a particular academic task and gets anxious and frustrated when asked to do so. If the problem behavior results in the child being put into a time out or being sent to the office, he or she can avoid the academic activity. Thus, an intended punishment is actually reinforcing the behavior. This category of function is often referred to as an "escape."

3. *Unable to perform the desired behavior.* The child has not acquired or become fluent in performing the desired social behavior that provides a desired result (either obtaining something or escape). In this situation, it makes sense that the child misbehaves given that he or she has not learned the desired behavior and is forced to engage in an alternative.

4. *Behavioral generalization.* In some cases, a child has not had to do a desired behavior in the manner or setting required in the current situation. For example, a child might have developed appropriate strategies to get the teacher's attention in the classroom, but needs to shift the behavior to be successful on the playground or lunchroom.

APPLICATION EXERCISE 3.2

Tina is a third-grade student with a learning disability in mathematics. This school year she is falling further behind in math. Her teacher reports that, during math, Tina often appears frustrated and is engaging in off-task and disruptive behaviors with increasing frequency (e.g., talking to peers about other topics, doing work from other subjects). She has good grades and behavior in other subject areas.

Challenge: Can you identify the core problem for Tina? What is the likely function of her problem behavior? How might this inform her integrated plan?

Discussion: Tina's primary problem appears to be academic, because her math struggles predate her behavior issues, which are limited to math class. She does not exhibit behavior problems in classes where she is not behind academically (as reported by her teacher; this could be confirmed with grades, screening data, discipline referral data, etc.). Misbehaving in math allows her to escape difficult math tasks (the hypothesized function of her behavior). Appropriate mathematics intervention may reasonably be expected to minimize problem behavior. Her integrated plan will focus on ensuring an academic match between her current skills and her math instruction and tasks to address escape behaviors, while working to improve her math skills so that she can eventually engage in grade-level tasks. Tina also might benefit from other motivational supports to encourage her to engage in math class despite her history of failure (e.g., Tina can participate in setting and monitoring her progress monitoring goals, so she feels she has control over her own success).

By focusing on functional explanations, we orient ourselves to factors external to the child that have been documented to impact academic and social behavior performance (e.g., positive feedback from the teacher, reinforcement for correct responding, a punishing task that leads to problem behavior). Because these factors can be directly manipulated, they support the identification of simple, practical targets for intervention programming. Pragmatically, behavior interventions are designed to focus on one or more of the hypothesized functions of the behavior. For example, noncontingent reinforcement is designed to provide a massive amount of teacher attention to a target child right at the beginning of the intervention period. This intervention would make sense to use in the case of a child whose problem behavior is hypothesized to be attention seeking. By providing the attention immediately, there is no reason for the child to engage in the problem behavior. As another example, consider a child who becomes highly disruptive when presented with a math task that he or she has significant difficulty successfully completing (high error rate). To test the hypothesis that the disruptive behavior is maintained by escape, we alter the task demand by lowering the difficulty of the math assignment, so that the child can complete it with few errors; if the hypothesis is correct, disruptive behavior will be reduced or eliminated by presenting a more appropriate academic task demand.

Using this model, a teacher or problem-solving team is asked to consider the most likely reasons for the problem behavior. Once a reason is determined, it can be used to select an intervention designed to address this function. While it is important for the team members to take care to make the best decision they can, the team should not unnecessarily delay intervention with prolonged hypothesis generation; we will test our hypotheses by implementing the intervention and monitoring its effectiveness (i.e., the student's response to the individualized intervention). This approach is effective only when coupled with timely intervention implementation and analysis. We only know the accuracy of the original hypothesis after the intervention is implemented and outcome data are analyzed, so it is important to collect and analyze progress monitoring data regularly, so that we can make any needed changes as quickly as possible. Thus, implementation of intervention with fidelity, collection of appropriate outcome data, and accurate analysis and decision making are essential components of the DBI process.

One important consideration when approaching functional assessment in schools is the amount of time allocated to assessment. Historically, functional assessment has been viewed as a very intense and time-consuming process, much like traditional psychometric assessment. Most school professionals can likely think of cases in which a functional assessment took weeks to complete. While there are certainly cases (e.g., children who are injuring themselves or others) in which it makes sense to spend a significant amount of time at the hypothesis generation stage, in most cases it makes more sense for this to be a rather brief review. The NCII (2013b) provides an excellent framework for "levels of analysis," ranging from informal to indirect/simple, to complex (see Table 3.2).

TABLE 3.2. Levels of Functional Analysis

Level	Data sources	Professionals involved
Informal	Archival review Problem-solving meeting	Teacher/staff
Indirect/simple	Functional assessment interview Functional behavioral assessment	Teacher/staff School specialist
Complex	Functional behavioral assessment Functional analysis	Teacher/staff School specialist Behavior-trained specialist

Using this three-tiered approach, as the problem behavior becomes more intense, or as we progress through the DBI process, the rigor of the sources of data increases and we start to include specialized, trained staff. For example, when we are first selecting behavioral strategies for an integrated plan, the informal level may be enough to hypothesize the function of behavior. If behavior worsens or does not respond to intervention, we may move to indirect/simple or even complex functional analysis to guide adaptations. In extreme cases, we may need to assess behavior and/or implement integrated intervention in controlled settings (rather than the natural environment) to pinpoint the function of behavior. For an in-depth training in this process we suggest *Using FBA for Diagnostic Assessment in Behavior (DBI Training Series Module 6; https://intensiveintervention. org/resource/using-fba-diagnostic-assessment-behavior-dbi-training-series-module-6)* from the NCII (2013b). The training materials include sample functional assessment interview forms, data collection forms, and functional assessment interviews.

APPLICATION EXERCISE 3.3

Simple functional assessment: Tina's teacher noted an increase in disruptive behavior and thought that this occurred predominantly in math class. To verify, she counted disruptive behavior across three classes for a week and graphed the counts separately (see Figure 3.2).

Challenge: What does this graph suggest about differences in Tina's behavior across settings? How does it inform the team's functional hypothesis? What other data could strengthen this hypothesis?

Discussion: These data verified that Tina's disruptive behavior occurred predominantly in math, supporting the hypothesis that such behavior serves to help her escape difficult math tasks. (Remember, with problem behaviors, lower levels and decreasing trends are the goal.) The team could further investigate this hypothesis by examining how often these behaviors resulted in task avoidance (e.g., time out, sent to office, change in task) and by seeing whether the behaviors decrease when Tina is presented with easier math tasks that she can complete successfully.

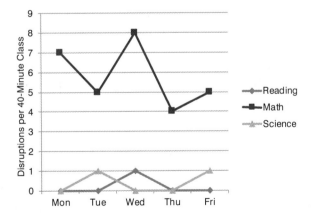

FIGURE 3.2. Tina's disruptive behavior in number of disruptions per 40-minute class (reading, math, and science), by class subject and day of the week for 1 week.

PROGRESS MONITORING

Once interventions are selected and implemented, it is essential to use progress monitoring tools to determine the impact on the desired outcome behavior. Given that intervention selection is simply a hypothesis generation exercise, the implementation, monitoring, and analysis stage provides the opportunity to discover whether the intervention is evidence based for the current child and situation. Graphs with goal lines and phase change lines (indicating intervention adaptions) are instrumental to this process, allowing us to make timely, data-based decisions and document what does and does not work for a given student. Graphs also are a great way to communicate with families (described more in a later section) and other staff members. For integrated plans, we must progress monitor in both academics and behavior to be sure the intervention is adequately addressing both areas of need. This section focuses on behavioral progress monitoring (see Pentimonti et al., Chapter 2, this volume, for a discussion of academic progress monitoring). While schools have made a great deal of progress in infusing academic progress monitoring into daily practice, there remains a dearth of behavior progress monitoring tools and use of those tools (Burns et al., 2012; Burns, Riley-Tillman, & Rathvon, 2017). Fortunately, this has been a focus of the NCII with the development of the Behavior Progress Monitoring Tools Chart (*https://intensiveintervention.org/chart/behavioral-progress-monitoring-tools*).

In this section, we highlight two behavior progress monitoring methods that are reliable, valid, and sensitive to change: momentary time sampling (MTS) and direct behavior rating (DBR; see ratings on the NCII Behavior Progress Monitoring Tools Chart). MTS, a form of systematic direct observation, involves the rating of student behavior at the end of predefined intervals of time. The version of MTS reviewed on the Tools Chart used 15-second intervals and focused on academic engagement defined by both active and passive engagement. At the end of the interval, the observer records whether the child is engaged at that moment; if so, the student gets "credit" for being engaged for the interval. This method can be combined with a variety of other versions of systematic direct observation (e.g., event recording) to provide a range of behavior progress monitoring options. For an excellent review of direct observation, see Briesch, Volpe, and Floyd (2018).

While MTS and other versions of systematic direct observation provide a valuable method of behavior progress monitoring, they typically require an external observer. In cases in which this is not an option, one can consider using DBR to monitor behavior. DBR combines aspects of behavior rating scales (teacher rating) and direct observation (recording right after the intervention period and repeated administration; Chafouleas, Riley-Tillman, & Christ, 2009; Christ, Riley-Tillman, & Chafouleas, 2009; Riley-Tillman, Chafouleas, & Briesch, 2007). The abbreviation DBR outlines the central features of the method. Specifically, DBR is Direct (ratings are collected immediately after the observation period), targets Behavior (rates behaviors such as Academic Engagement, Disruptive Behavior, and Respectful), and involves Rating (based on the rater's perception of the target behavior). Using DBR, a teacher can record whether a child is, for example, engaged and/or disruptive while a behavior intervention is in place. By recording over time, and plotting ratings against intervention changes, the teacher can determine which supports are associated with the best behavior. A great deal of research has accumulated for DBR scales, resulting in DBR for Academic Engagement and Disruptive Behavior being rated by NCII as valid, reliable, and sensitive to change. For more information on DBR, see *http://dbr.education.uconn.edu.*

While behavior progress monitoring data can be used in a similar manner to academic progress monitoring, there are a few important considerations. First, as mentioned in Table 3.1, behavioral progress monitoring outcomes tend to change much more quickly than their academic counterpart. Particularly in cases where the child has already acquired the desired behavior, if said behavior is appropriately supported (e.g., positively reinforced), there should be an immediate increase in that behavior. As a result, while we typically progress monitor for weeks prior to considering whether an academic intervention is working, behavioral outcome data can show much more immediate effects (Riley-Tillman, Burns, & Gibbons, 2013). In addition to the focus on immediate change, behavioral progress monitoring data are often highly variable. In some instances, the desired outcome will simply be to reduce variability and more consistently see the appropriate behavior. Because of this variability, we sometimes need to extend the baseline phase to provide a full understanding of the range of the behavior prior to the intervention. Finally, while academic behavior (e.g., reading fluency) is often consistent across environments, it is expected that behavior will change across settings. As a result, it is very important to consider behavioral progress monitoring data within the context of the setting where the observation occurred.

APPLICATION EXERCISE 3.4

Challenge: Jeremy's science teacher used DBR to rate his academic engagement for 3 days (see Figure 3.3). What do these baseline data tell us?

Discussion: With only these three data points, it is hard to tell whether Jeremy's engagement is highly variable or might be improving over time. The teacher collected data for the rest of the week (see Figure 3.4) and decided that Jeremy's engagement was highly variable but generally low and not increasing, never reaching 50%.

WHAT DO I DO LONG TERM?

The steps of diagnostic/functional assessment, integrated planning and adaptation, and progress monitoring in both academics and behavior continue until the student is meeting his or her goals in both areas. As students make progress, you should consider fading supports. This lets you use school resources and your time as efficiently as possible, and allows the student to function as independently as possible, which is an important long-term consideration. You will likely initially begin by gradually fading supports for the secondary problem, continuing to monitor progress to verify that the

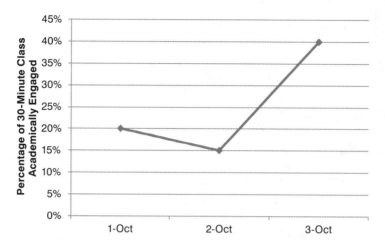

FIGURE 3.3. Baseline data for Jeremy's academic engaged time during science class, expressed as the percentage of the 30-minute class in which Jeremy was academically engaged across 3 consecutive days.

student maintains his or her progress. If academic progress slows or behavior worsens, you will need to increase supports back to a level at which the student maintains previous gains. When possible, you also will try fading supports in the primary area. It is important to note, however, that when students have intensive needs, you may not be able to fully fade supports. Even when the student does seem to maintain without intervention, you should continue to monitor periodically. It is important that you document everything you have tried, and how the student responded to each approach, so that future teachers and teams do not have to repeat unsuccessful approaches if problems recur or worsen.

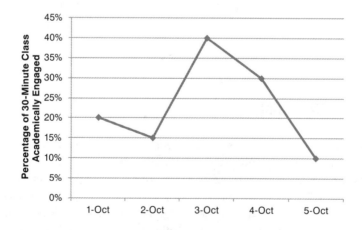

FIGURE 3.4. Extended baseline data for Jeremy's academic engaged time during science class, expressed as the percentage of the 30-minute class in which Jeremy was academically engaged across 5 consecutive days.

APPLICATION EXERCISE 3.5

Progress monitoring through adaptation and fading: The following graph tracks Jeremy's science engagement. During baseline week, his engagement never exceeded 40%. The team designed an intensive intervention plan that included behavioral prompts and rewards for increased engagement. His science teacher implemented both components the following week and monitored his engagement compared to a goal of 80%, also plotting his weekly quiz grades. The goal of 80% was selected as a feasible improvement over baseline that would bring his engagement closer to that of his peers; note that perfect (100%) engagement is not the goal, because it is not realistic and is not required to make Jeremy more successful in science class.

As seen in Figure 3.5, Jeremy's engagement improved compared to baseline, but he never reached the goal during the first week of intervention. The team adapted his plan to provide more academic support in science and changed his reinforcement plan (allowing him to more easily earn a reward that he could select from a menu). During this adaptation phase, Jeremy's engagement improved until he was consistently meeting and usually exceeding the goal. His weekly quiz scores also improved. After the third week of this plan, the team decided to reduce the teacher's behavioral prompts and the reinforcement schedule.

Challenge: What happened during the first week of fading? What would you recommend?

Discussion: During the first week of fading, Jeremy's academic engagement dipped. While his engagement was still higher than during baseline or his first intensive plan, he was not doing as well as he did under the adapted plan. His average engagement dropped, and he only met the goal once. He also scored lower on the quiz than during recent weeks. The team should his increase his supports (prompts or reinforcement or both), returning to the full adapted plan if needed.

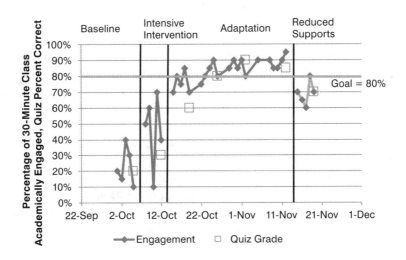

FIGURE 3.5. Jeremy's academic engaged time progress monitoring data and quiz scores over multiple phases: baseline, intensive intervention, adapted intensive intervention, and reduced supports. Engagement is expressed as the percentage of the 30-minute class in which Jeremy was academically engaged. Quiz score is expressed as percent correct. The goal is 80% for both engagement and quiz scores.

COMMUNICATING WITH PARENTS AND FAMILIES

Parents can provide important insights into students' academic and behavioral history; they may be particularly helpful in developing functional hypotheses by describing past behavior and behavior in nonschool settings. They also may be able to support intervention implementation by helping students generalize desired behaviors in other settings or providing reinforcement at home. Therefore, we ideally want to engage parents in intensive intervention planning, implementation, and monitoring whenever possible. When doing so, we must be careful to avoid jargon, especially regarding functional or diagnostic assessment. In addition, it is important to talk about children's behavior as something that makes sense given the environment, rather than as something from within the child. This approach is less stigmatizing for the child and helps the parents think about how best to consider behavior issues in the home environment. Finally, we have found that graphed data may help parents better understand students' progress, including why changes in supports are sometimes needed. A simple AB line graph allows both educational professionals and partners to see where a child performed prior to intervention (A; baseline) and where they perform with intervention (B). Vertical phase lines and labels can indicate when adaptations occur, as seen in Jeremy's graph in Application Exercise 3.5. Plotting academic and behavioral data on the same graph (as seen in Application Exercise 3.5), or showing two graphs side by side, can indicate how the two areas are interrelated. This graphical information can provide a clear presentation of the child's performance, whereas a narrative can easily be mistaken by the parent as either more positive or more negative than the actual situation.

CONSIDERATIONS AT MIDDLE AND HIGH SCHOOL

Some of the considerations for middle and high school that were discussed in previous chapters apply to integrated academic/behavioral plans. These differences compared to elementary school settings occur at both the school level (e.g., staff roles and responsibilities, class structures and schedules, graduation requirements) and the student level (e.g., more severe academic deficits or more extreme behaviors). Implementing DBI to address behavior makes schedules particularly important to consider, as students will likely need support across settings. When behavior varies across settings, supports may need to vary across settings and educators, too, requiring a more nuanced plan. Teams may have to coordinate with more staff members to determine whether function varies across settings, adjust the plan to each setting, support staff members in implementing the plan in each setting, and monitor behavior in all relevant settings. As with academic problems, long-standing behavioral problems may be more entrenched and resistant to change in higher grades.

Pentimonti et al. (Chapter 2, this volume) discussed how academic screening and progress monitoring may be more challenging in later grades due to the reduced availability of validated tools. This may be less of a concern for behavior. While there are fewer tools available in behavior, they often can be used across grades (e.g., systematic direct observation, DBR). Similarly, many behavioral strategies can be applied across grades, although they need to be age appropriate. For example, while positive reinforcement may be used at any age, students will likely desire different things at different ages; smiley face stickers may motivate some young children but would not be expected to motivate a high school student. As always, we must consider what motivates each student and adjust accordingly. Older students may be better able to take an active part in identifying their needs (e.g., by participating in functional interviews), planning their supports, and taking an active role in implementation and monitoring (e.g., behavior contracts, learning to request breaks or supports, self-monitoring behavior, or academic task completion and performance).

SUMMARY

Guidance provided in this chapter can support teachers as they consider both academic and behavioral needs in designing and monitoring integrated intensive intervention. For more information on this topic, we recommend reviewing the modules located at the NCII website that are focused on behavioral or integrated intervention (see Appendix 3.1). In addition to outlining the theory for academic and behavior intervention selection, implementation, and monitoring, these modules present a variety of helpful tools. Finally, when looking for evidence-based intervention options for behavior problems, consider reviewing the Evidence-Based Intervention (EBI) Network (*ebi.missouri.edu*), which has an extensive list of behavior interventions sorted by function to aid in selection. As previously mentioned, NCII has tools charts for both academic and behavioral interventions.

Although integrated academic and behavioral intervention likely will require more work than addressing the primary need in isolation, it will be more effective than leaving an area of need unaddressed. We all have seen situations in which good academic intervention is ineffective due to behavior issues. Similarly, behavior intervention alone will not work if the student is misbehaving because he or she cannot keep up academically. The extra effort and time put into integrated planning may yield stronger and timelier changes in both academic and behavior outcomes.

FREQUENTLY ASKED QUESTIONS

My school doesn't have a behavioral progress monitoring tool. What can I do?

Some validated behavioral progress monitoring methods, such as systematic direct observation and DBR, are free to use. For more information, see the NCII Behavioral Progress Monitoring Tools Chart (*https://intensiveintervention.org/chart/behavioral-progress-monitoring-tools*) and the modules and webinars listed in the Resources in Appendix 3.1.

I'm not a behavior expert, who can help me develop a functional hypothesis?

Schools often have staff with behavioral expertise, such as school psychologists, social workers, or a special education teacher or behavior interventionist trained in applied behavioral analysis. NCII has resources to support informal functional assessment, including *Using FBA for Diagnostic Assessment in Behavior (DBI Professional Learning Series Module 6)* and the brief guide *Ask Clarifying Questions to Create a Hypothesis to Guide Intervention Changes*. Links to these and other resources are in Appendix 3.1.

Why should I graph data?

Graphs with goal lines and phase change lines (indicating intervention adaptations) allow us to make timely data-based decisions about when we need to change a student's supports. They also document what does and does not work for a given student. Graphs also are a great way to communicate with families and other school staff about a child's progress and why supports sometimes need to be changed.

How long should I wait before making an intervention change?

First, you must give the intervention enough time to work. Academic skills will likely take a few weeks to show a change. Behavior change may occur more quickly, especially if the student does not have to learn new behaviors. We also must collect enough progress monitoring data that we are confident in the stability and trend of our data. For academics, Christ and Silberglitt (2007) recommend six to nine data points. With weekly progress monitoring, you might wait a month and a half or 2 months before deciding whether you need to change the intervention. For behavior, you may only need three to five (see the video *For students with intensive behavior needs, how many data points are needed to make decisions?* at *https://intensiveintervention.org/resource/students-intensive-behavior-needs-how-many-data-points-are-needed-make-decisions*).

How does this interface with MTSS/PBIS?

Intensive intervention is the most intensive support provided in MTSS or positive behavior interventions and supports (PBIS) (e.g., Tier 3 in a three-tiered model). With integrated supports, the academic and behavioral components may fall at different tiers. For example, a student with intensive behavioral needs but less severe reading needs may have an intensive, individualized behavior plan and participate in a Tier 2 reading group.

REFERENCES

Berry Kuchle, L., Zumeta Edmonds, R., Danielson, L. C., Peterson, A., & Riley-Tillman, T. C. (2015). The next big idea: A framework for integrated academic and behavioral intensive intervention. *Learning Disabilities Research and Practice, 30,* 150–158.

Briesch, A. M., Volpe, R. J., & Floyd, R. G. (2018). *School-based observation: A practical guide to assessing student behavior.* New York: Guilford Press.

Burns, M. K., Riley-Tillman, T. C., & Rathvon, N. (2017). *Effective school interventions: Evidence-based strategies for improving student outcomes* (3rd ed.). New York: Guilford Press.

Burns, M. K., Riley-Tillman, T. C., & VanDerHeyden, A. (2012). *Response to intervention applications: Vol. 1. Academic and behavioral interventions.* New York: Guilford Press.

Chafouleas, S. M., Riley-Tillman, T. C., & Christ, T. J. (2009). Direct behavior rating (DBR): An emerging method for assessing social behavior within a tiered intervention system. *Assessment for Effective Intervention, 34,* 195–200.

Christ, T. J., Riley-Tillman, T. C., & Chafouleas, S. M. (2009). Foundation for the development and use of direct behavior rating (DBR) to Assess and Evaluate Student Behavior. *Assessment for Effective Intervention, 34,* 201–213.

Christ, T. J., & Silberglitt, B. (2007). Estimates of the standard error of measurement for curriculum-based measures of oral reading fluency. *School Psychology Review, 36,* 130–146.

McFarland, J., Hussar, B., de Brey, C., Snyder, T., Wang, X., Wilkinson-Flicker, S., . . . Hinz, S. (2017). *The condition of education 2017* (NCES 2017-144). Washington, DC: National Center for Education Statistics. Retrieved from *https://nces.ed.gov/pubs2017/2017144.pdf.*

National Center on Intensive Intervention. (2013a). *Data-based individualization: A framework for intensive intervention.* Washington, DC: Office of Special Education, U.S. Department of Education. Retrieved from *www.intensiveintervention.org/resource/data-based-individualization-framework-intensive-intervention.*

National Center on Intensive Intervention. (2013b). *Using FBA for diagnostic assessment in behavior.* Washington, DC: U.S. Department of Education, Office of Special Education Programs, National Center on Intensive Intervention. Retrieved from *https://intensiveintervention.org/resource/using-fba-diagnostic-assessment-behavior-dbi-training-series-module-6.*

Riley-Tillman, T. C., Burns, M. K., & Gibbons, K. (2013). *Response to intervention applications: Vol. 2. Assessment, design and decision making.* New York: Guilford Press.

Riley-Tillman, T. C., Chafouleas, S. M., & Briesch, A. M. (2007). A school practitioner's guide to using Daily Behavior Report Cards to monitor interventions. *Psychology in the Schools, 44,* 77–89.

Sanford, C., Newman, L., Wagner, M., Cameto, R., Knokey, A.-M., & Shaver, D. (2011). The post-high school outcomes of young adults with disabilities up to 6 years after high school: Key findings from the National Longitudinal Transition Study–2 (NLTS2) (NCSER 2011-3004). Retrieved from *www.ies.ed.gov/ncser/pubs/20113004/pdf/20113004.pdf.*

Resources

This summary reflects resources available as of February 2019. New resources will likely become available in the future and website reorganization may change links.

Student Meeting Tools

- **Tools to Support Intensive Intervention Data Meetings.** Premeeting, initial meeting, and progress monitoring meeting protocols (guides, agendas, templates, etc.) to support data team meetings for students receiving intensive intervention. *https://intensiveintervention.org/implementation-support/ tools-support-intensive-intervention-data-meetings*
- **Ask Clarifying Questions to Create a Hypothesis to Guide Intervention Changes.** Questions to help teams analyze data and develop a hypothesis to guide intervention planning (e.g., skills deficit, function of behavior). *https://intensiveintervention.org/sites/default/files/ Ask_Clarifying_Questions_Hypothesis-Question_Bank_Handout.pdf*

Intervention Resources

Tools Chart

- **Behavioral Intervention Tools Chart.** Reviews studies about behavioral interventions. *https://charts.intensiveintervention.org/chart/behavioral-intervention-chart*

Resources

- **Behavior Strategies to Support Intensifying Interventions.** Developed for classroom teachers to use with students who may require academic and/or behavioral support. Include intensification strategies for students with more intensive behaviors. *https://intensiveintervention.org/intervention-resources/behavior-strategies-support-intensifying-interventions*
  - Self-Management
  - Antecedent Modification
  - Reinforcement Strategy
  - Behavior Contracts
  - Point Sheets/Behavior Report Card
  - Classroom Conversations and Participation
  - Intermittent Reinforcement Using a Timer
  - The "You–Me" Game
  - Yes/No Learning Skills Chart
- **Intensification Strategy Checklist.** Strategies for intensifying or adapting intensive intervention. *https://intensiveintervention.org/sites/default/files/Intensification_Strategy_Checklist_Handout-2018.docx*

Webinars

- **Bringing It Together: Why It Is Important to Integrate Academics and Behavior When Thinking about Intensive Intervention—September 2015.** Discusses the integrated relationship between academics and behavior, reviews a case study example using DBI to provide individualized integrated academic and behavioral support based on student need, and shares behavioral strategies intended to support teachers working with students with primary academic deficits and challenging behaviors. *https://intensiveintervention.org/resource/bringing-it-together-why-it-important-integrate-academics-and-behavior-when-thinking-about*

(continued)

- **What Is an Evidence-Based Behavior Intervention? Choosing and Implementing Behavior Interventions That Work—June 2014.** Discusses considerations for selecting and using evidence-based interventions to address challenging behaviors. The webinar introduces NCII's new Behavior Interventions Tools Chart and describes how educators can best utilize this resource and other available resources to select interventions. *https://intensiveintervention.org/resource/what-evidence-based-behavior-intervention-choosing-and-implementing-behavior-interventions*
- **Providing Intensive Intervention Using Data-Based Individualization in Behavior—January 2013.** Describes the essential components of the DBI process while highlighting a relevant student example in behavior, providing a good foundational understanding of how interventions can be intensified and individualized for students with persistent behavioral challenges. *https://intensiveintervention.org/resource/providing-intensive-intervention-using-data-based-individualization-behavior*

Training Module

- **What Do I Do Now? Individualizing Behavior Interventions When Standard Approaches Don't Work (DBI Professional Learning Series Module 8).** Focuses primarily on selecting evidence-based interventions that align with the functions of behavior for students with severe and persistent learning and behavior needs. *https://intensiveintervention.org/resource/what-do-i-do-now-individualizing-behavior-interventions-when-standard-approaches-dont-work*
  - Handout 1: Story of Evidence-Based Interventions
  - Handout 2: Tier 3 Planning Checklist
  - Handout 3: Examples of Evidence-Based Interventions
  - Handout 4: Linking Assessment and Monitoring

Assessment Resources

Tools Chart

- **Behavioral Progress Monitoring Tools Chart.** Presents information about behavior progress monitoring tools. *https://charts.intensiveintervention.org/chart/behavioral-progress-monitoring-tools*

Direct Behavior Ratings

- DBR involves rating of behavior, following a specified observation period, then sharing that information to inform decisions. *http://dbr.education.uconn.edu*

Modules

- **Monitoring Student Progress for Behavioral Interventions (DBI Professional Learning Series Module 3).** Focuses on behavioral progress monitoring within the context of the DBI process and addresses (1) methods available for behavioral progress monitoring, including but not limited to DBR, and (2) using progress monitoring data to make decisions about behavioral interventions. *https://intensiveintervention.org/resource/monitoring-student-progress-behavioral-interventions-dbi-training-series-module-3*
  - Handout 1: Student Qualification Sheet
  - Handout 2: Target Behavior Questionnaire
  - Handout 3: ABC Checklist
  - Handout 4: Anecdotal Recording Form

(continued)

- ○ Handout 5: Target Behavior Definition Practice
- ○ Handout 6: Direct Behavior Rating Individualization Form
- ○ NCII DBR Graphing Template
- **Using FBA for Diagnostic Assessment in Behavior (DBI Professional Learning Series Module 6).** Serves as an introduction to important concepts and processes for implementing functional behavioral assessment (FBA), including behavior basics such as reinforcement and punishment. *https://intensiveintervention.org/resource/using-fba-diagnostic-assessment-behavior-dbi-training-series-module-6*
  - ○ Handout 1: FBA and Behavior Support Plan Self Assessment
  - ○ Handout 2: Common Problem Behaviors
  - ○ Handout 3a: Functional Behavior Assessment Process
  - ○ Handout 3b: Functional Assessment Interview
  - ○ Handout 3c: ABC Report Form
  - ○ Handout 3d: Positive Behavior Support Plan Worksheet
  - ○ Handout 4: ABC Report Form Example

Webinar

- **Monitoring Student Progress for Behavioral Interventions—April 2013.** Discusses how to measure behavior more systematically with a focus on (1) defining progress monitoring; (2) methods available for progress monitoring, including but not limited to DBR; and (3) ways to examine progress monitoring data and make decisions about instruction and behavioral interventions. *https://intensiveintervention.org/resource/monitoring-student-progress-behavioral-interventions*

CHAPTER 4

Intensive Intervention for Students with Intellectual and Developmental Disabilities

CHRISTOPHER J. LEMONS
SAMANTHA A. GESEL
LAUREN M. LEJEUNE

GUIDING QUESTIONS

➤ Is intensive intervention appropriate for students with intellectual and developmental disabilities?

➤ How would a special education teacher integrate data-based individualization into services for a student with intellectual and developmental disabilities?

➤ What are additional considerations when implementing data-based individualization with students with intellectual and developmental disabilities?

During the 40 years that schools in the United States have been legally required to provide a free and appropriate public education to students with disabilities, the expectations regarding the focus of this education for students with intellectual and developmental disabilities (IDD) and the level of literacy they should obtain have drastically changed. Recent studies demonstrate that students with IDD are able to achieve reading levels that are substantially higher than what would have been expected merely 20 years ago (Allor, Mathes, Roberts, Cheatham, & Al Otaiba, 2014; Lemons et al., 2013). Data-based individualization (DBI) is a process that can assist special educators in improving the reading outcomes of their students in alignment with these new expectations. We encourage teachers of students with IDD to consider integrating intensive intervention through DBI into the special education services they provide.

This recommendation is especially relevant in light of the March 2017 *Endrew F. v. Douglas County School District* Supreme Court decision. In this decision, the Court upheld the mandate of the Individuals with Disabilities Education Act (IDEA) to see that educational programs are reasonably designed to ensure that students with disabilities demonstrate appropriate progress. This ruling is important, because it clarified the standard for designing individualized education program (IEP) goals and corresponding intervention plans that provide opportunities for meaningful growth, beyond "merely more than de minimis" (*Endrew F. v. Douglas County School District,* 2017). In fact, Turnbull, Turnbull, and Cooper (2018) stated that "to achieve *Endrew's* aims, teachers will need to make timely and evidence-based decisions regarding students' progress toward ambitious goals and objectives" (p. 136). In order for children and adolescents with IDD to reach their fullest potential, school staff members need to ensure that the IEP is designed and implemented with highest level of rigor. DBI is a process perfectly aligned with the type of IEP envisioned in *Endrew.* Incorporating DBI into the IEP increases the likelihood that students with IDD demonstrate meaningful progress.

Our purpose in this chapter is to provide guidance to special education teachers of students with IDD on integrating DBI into their special education services. We included a chapter with this focus in this book because a majority of the guidance on DBI implementation to date has focused on students with high-incidence disabilities (i.e., learning disability, emotional disturbance). Despite this fact, DBI is a highly appropriate process that has potential to substantially improve educational outcomes of students with IDD. Our hope is that this chapter will highlight areas in which minor adjustments to currently available guidance may be necessary to meet the needs of learners with IDD and, consequently, help special education teachers understand how to implement DBI with students from this population. Note that although our example is focused on literacy, DBI is also appropriate to implement in other academic content areas (e.g., mathematics).

Before reading this chapter, we encourage you to familiarize yourself with the introduction and first chapter of this book. Doing so will make certain that you have an understanding of why intensive intervention is necessary for many students with disabilities and that you are familiar with the steps of implementing DBI. As a reminder, DBI is an iterative process by which interventionists use data to adapt and intensify academic and behavioral interventions for students who are demonstrating inadequate response to intervention (see Peterson, Danielson, & Fuchs, Chapter 1, this volume). DBI can be included in the most intensive tier of intervention in response-to-intervention (RTI) or multi-tiered systems of support (MTSS) frameworks, and DBI is a process that should also be incorporated into special education service delivery.

To help teachers of students with IDD understand how to apply the guidance provided throughout this book, we use a vignette that focuses on Millie, an 8-year-old third grader with Down syndrome (DS), and the decisions that her IEP team members make during DBI implementation. After briefly introducing you to Millie, we highlight important considerations for educators to contemplate as they implement DBI with children and adolescents with IDD. This information is provided to expand on the guidance provided in the initial chapters of this book. We then return to the vignette to provide a concrete example of what DBI implementation could look like for a student with IDD. Finally, we conclude with two application exercises that give you an opportunity to practice using the information you learned while reading this chapter.

INTRODUCING MILLIE

Millie began receiving early intervention services shortly after birth, and she qualified for special education services when she turned 3 years old. With a reported IQ score of 45, Millie has a moderate intellectual disability. Millie speaks in complete sentences but makes articulation errors that lead to frustration at times. Task persistence is a challenge for Millie, particularly as task difficulty increases. Millie's IEP includes goals in reading, mathematics, and language.

Millie's mother, Ms. Ryder, is actively involved with the planning of her daughter's education. Recently, Ms. Ryder attended a research conference sponsored by Down Syndrome Indiana. At this conference, she heard several speakers describe research on enhancing reading outcomes for children with DS. These presentations resonated with Ms. Ryder, who has recently been concerned about the limited reading progress her daughter has made over her first several years in elementary school. She wondered whether Millie might benefit from a shift in her reading instruction. Ms. Ryder spent some time reading over conference handouts and exploring several of the websites recommended by the speakers. After careful consideration, Ms. Ryder decided that she wished to share these resources with Millie's IEP team to discuss Millie's reading instruction and the possibility of intensifying it using DBI. She sent Millie's special education teacher, Ms. Purser, an e-mail to explain her thoughts and to request a meeting to further discuss them with the IEP team.

CONSIDERATIONS FOR IMPLEMENTING DBI WITH STUDENTS WITH IDD

Special educators of children and adolescents with IDD can use the DBI process described in the opening chapters of this book to effectively intensify interventions for children and adolescents with IDD. However, additional considerations may be necessary as the iterative process of intervention–assessment–adaptation is applied to this population of learners. We highlight several of these areas of consideration next, followed by presentation of a concrete example of implementing DBI with a student with IDD.

Assessment

One of the greatest challenges in implementing typical DBI guidance with learners with IDD relates to assessment. Some of the many questions include the following: Which measures do we use? How frequently do we administer these? How frequently do we make instructional adaptations? Applying current recommendations of administering weekly curriculum-based measurement (CBM; Deno, 1985) probes and making changes after 4 consecutive weeks of data below a student's aimline are often not appropriate for many children and adolescents with IDD. Many students with IDD need longer periods of intervention to make progress that is measurable on CBM. Because of this, teachers will likely need to be more flexible as they consider the needs of each student and rely more on professional judgment. We recommend that teachers consider a comprehensive assessment plan that integrates both CBM and informal assessments including teacher observations and curriculum-aligned measures. We encourage teachers to maintain the initial focus of instruction for about 6–8 weeks before making substantial changes to the plan. However, if informal assessment indicates challenges related to behavior (e.g., engagement, motivation), we suggest that teachers should make necessary adaptations to support their student in engaging with the instructional content. We provide an example of being flexible with assessment in the vignette.

Behavior

In many ways, challenging behavior of students with IDD is the metaphorical elephant in the room. Teachers and parents are aware of this challenge. However, too frequently it is not discussed in initial stages of planning academic intervention. Importantly, after the *Endrew* Supreme Court decision, "programs that do not address a student's behavior, when the student's behavior affects other progress, are also no longer acceptable" (Turnbull et al., 2018, p. 132). Behavioral support is included as one dimension of the taxonomy of intervention intensity, a guide to help educators consider various ways to increase intervention intensity (Fuchs, Fuchs, & Malone, 2017; see Table 4.1 and discussion in Chapter 1, this volume). Thus, it is essential for special educators who are designing DBI for children and adolescents with IDD to ensure that sufficient attention is devoted to behavioral supports during the initial planning phases. Most (if not all) students with IDD have needs in the areas of engagement, motivation, perseverance, and compliance. Interventionists who design and implement an intensive intervention plan that does not account for behavioral supports likely will have to quickly redesign the plan to provide behavioral support. We recommend that special education teachers seek out consultation and support from behavior specialists to adequately consider behavioral aspects of the intervention during the initial planning stages of DBI, thus improving the potential effectiveness of interventions by matching it to the specific learner profile.

Students with Complex Communication Needs

Many students with IDD have accompanying difficulties with expressive language or articulation. Several of these students might be classified as having complex communication needs. In other words, they are students who need additional communication supports beyond speech production to allow them to communicate clearly during instruction. We encourage teachers of students with complex communication needs to involve related service providers, including the speech–language pathologist and alternative and augmentative communication (AAC) specialist, in initial planning. Adaptations to support students' communication needs will likely need to be applied to both the delivery of instruction and the assessment of student learning. These adaptations may be incorporated into the initial DBI plan or they may be added later if response to the initial plan is not adequate. Additionally, communication targets may be incorporated into the goals of instruction. Lower-tech (e.g., picture cards) and higher-tech (e.g., tablets, computers) options are available to allow students to provide responses by selecting images and words from an array of available choices.

Involving Family Members

Parents, siblings, and other family members of children and adolescents with IDD can offer valuable support during DBI implementation. Although IDEA requires parents to participate in the IEP process, in our experience, this involvement is often limited. We encourage special educators who are implementing DBI to reconsider the role of family members. First, family members and the student (when appropriate) should be involved in setting goals. This is critical for students with IDD, who may take multiple years to make substantial progress. Family members who can provide insight on previous goals, interventions, and student response can ensure that the IEP includes goals that are ambitious, realistic, and meaningful to the family. It is critical that special educators communicate frequently with family members regarding the student's response. It is important that data are described in an understandable way and that all involved celebrate successes along the way.

Second, family members may be able to provide insight into student preferences or interest that may be used to guide adaptations to intervention. For example, family members could identify reinforcing activities that may increase a student's willingness to attempt challenging work, and they can share preferred topics that could guide the alignment of instructional content with the student's interest. Third, in our experience, many families are interested in supporting school interventions at home. In academics, this may mean reviewing recently learned material; in behavior, it may mean aligning the home behavior management plan with the school's plan. We encourage special educators to discuss family members' desires and capacity to support DBI at home. Relatedly, special educators are also in a good position to share resources (e.g., parent support groups) that may increase family members' capacity to support their child with IDD in the home.

Inclusion

Including students with IDD in instruction and activities with same-age peers who do not have disabilities is both a priority in IDEA and valuable for academic and social gains for students with and without disabilities. This having been said, there are meaningful barriers to implementing DBI in a general education classroom. Special educators and IEP team members should discuss goals and priorities during the IEP meeting. For many students with IDD, it is likely that some period of time outside of the general education setting will be needed for instruction to be delivered with sufficient intensity to achieve goals. Consider a third-grade student with IDD who is substantially below grade level. It is unlikely that a general educator who is delivering instruction to a full classroom of third graders would also be able to provide this student with instruction and behavior support that is as intensive and individualized as services provided outside of the general education classroom by a special education teacher and paraeducator. IEP teams implementing DBI must carefully consider the best way to balance a student's time spent in inclusive settings along with opportunities to receive services that are sufficiently intensive to meaningfully impact academic and behavioral outcomes.

TABLE 4.1. Fuchs, Fuchs, and Malone's Dimensions of Intervention Intensity

Question	Explanation	Relevance to students with IDD
Strength		
Is there evidence from experimental studies that the validated intervention program is effective for students like my target student?	• "Evidence" differs based on study design. • Randomized control trials (RCTs): "Strength" based on effect size (ES), which compares students who received treatment to those who did not. Larger ES indicate stronger intervention effects. ES interpretations include 0.25 to 0.35 (small, value-added); 0.35 to 0.40 (moderate); >0.50 (large). • Single-case design (SCD) studies: "Strength" based on evidence of a functional relation (FR) between the intervention and the dependent variable. This is determined by considering immediacy and consistency of effect, presence of overlapping data across phases, and changes in the level, trend, and variability of data.	• Research involving students with IDD typically uses SCD, since IDD is a low-incidence disability and it is more challenging to recruit a larger number of participants for an RCT. • With SCD, you should consider the profiles of study participants and how they are similar (or dissimilar) to your students. Study results may be most likely to replicate if you choose interventions that are validated for students similar to your students.
Dosage		
Are there increased opportunities for the target student to respond and receive corrective feedback compared to previous interventions?	• You may achieve increased opportunities by reducing group size and increasing intervention duration and/or frequency, relative to previous remediation attempts.	• Teachers of students with IDD can increase dosage by involving other instructors (i.e., paraeducators) or related-services staff (i.e., speech–language pathologist).
Alignment		
Does the intervention adequately address the target student's academic deficit needs and support learning of (or progress toward) grade-appropriate academic standards?	• Ensuring that an intervention is closely aligned with student's learning needs decreases the need for future adaptations. A solid understanding of current levels of performance is needed to select an appropriate intervention.	• Many students with IDD demonstrate splinter skills (e.g., deficits in foundational skills but competence in more advanced tasks). Therefore, special educators may need to select intervention components from more than one program to serve as the validated intervention platform.
Attention to transfer		
Is the intervention designed to help students transfer skills they learn to other formats and contexts and to realize connections between mastered and related skills?	• It is appropriate to focus interventions on specific skill-deficits, but you should set ultimate goals to improve students' skills more broadly. • Interventions are more successful when they provide strategic tools that students can use beyond specific sessions.	• Students with IDD may have difficulty transferring skills to other formats, contexts, and related skills. • Special educators should align intervention goals with grade-level academic standards to maximize overlap in instructional language/content and,

76

	• Teachers can support transfer by explicitly modeling how skills relate to other formats (e.g., CBMs with skills similar to instruction), contexts (e.g., the general education classroom), and skills (e.g., applying phonics instruction to a decodable text).	consequently, students' ability to transfer skills beyond the immediate intervention context.
Comprehensiveness Does the intervention incorporate many principles of explicit instruction?	• We outlined principles of explicit instruction in our section on deciding to implement DBI. • Fuchs et al. suggest that instructors consider the presence (or absence) of simple/direct language, modeling of strategies, use of background knowledge, gradual release of responsibility, guided and independent practice opportunities, and systematic review.	• Explicit instruction is essential to ensuring that students with IDD master taught content. • Teachers can make instruction even more explicit by increasing real-life applicability and using manipulative or other concrete representations of abstract skills.
Behavior supports Does the intervention incorporate self-regulation, executive function components, and behavioral principles to minimize problem behavior?	• Children often exhibit concurrent academic and behavior difficulties. There is not a clear causal explanation for this, since academic and behavioral challenges can build on each other and create a negative cycle of poor outcomes. • Incorporate behavioral supports in academic interventions to maximize the extent to which students participate in and learn from their intervention program.	• Students with IDD respond best to academic interventions that incorporate behavioral strategies. • Constant or progressive time delay and system of least prompts can proactively support student behaviors that may increase due to task difficulty. • Additional supports may be necessary for more challenging problem behaviors (e.g., aggression or elopement). Collaborate with a behavioral specialist to create an individualized behavior plan.
Individualization Have you created a plan for individualizing the intervention based on student response?	• Some students will continue to show inadequate growth even when they receive a validated intervention program that addresses the first six dimensions. Therefore, individualization is a core component of DBI. • A teacher implementing DBI should write out the details of the intervention plan, including the steps for monitoring student progress, making decisions about student response to intervention, and a step-by-step guide to planning adaptations. • Document these plans and share them with team members to increase the likelihood for adequate follow-through.	• Students with IDD will likely show slower growth in academic skills than students with other disabilities, but they *do* learn with the correct combination of academic and behavioral supports. • Document the specific details of your students' DBI plan to prevent a prolonged period of nonresponse to intervention.

Note. See Fuchs, Fuchs, and Malone (2017) for a more thorough description of each of these dimensions and an applied example of each dimension in action.

Middle and High School (and Beyond)

Special education researchers know somewhat less about how DBI may work for students with IDD beyond the elementary grades. We hypothesize that the process would look quite similar in middle and high school, at least as it relates to instruction in basic skills such as reading and math. As with most interventions for older learners, interventionists need to consider using age-appropriate instructional materials. Additionally, as students get closer to age 21, the IEP team, including the family members and the student, need to balance the instructional focus on basic skills with the skills necessary to successfully transition into postsecondary settings. We also recommend that many college-based postsecondary programs consider how to integrate DBI into their efforts to enhance academic skills of students. As Wei, Blackorby, and Schiller (2011) have demonstrated, the developmental trajectory of reading and math growth for students with IDD continues to increase through the high school years. Thus, it is likely that many students with IDD in postsecondary settings would continue to benefit from intensive, individualized intervention in reading and math.

RETURNING TO IMPLEMENTATION OF DBI WITH MILLIE

The considerations we have highlighted indicate that special educators implementing DBI with students with IDD will likely face additional challenges and decisions compared to special educators who are teaching children with high-incidence disabilities (e.g., learning disability). Next, we return to our vignette in which we follow Millie, her mother, and school personnel as they implement DBI. We encourage special educators who decide to integrate DBI into their services to consult the opening chapters of this book for additional ideas and resources.

Deciding to Change Millie's Instruction

At the start of kindergarten, Millie could read only her name. She was included full time in the general education classroom in kindergarten and first grade. Beginning in second grade, Millie began receiving supplemental one-on-one reading instruction from a paraprofessional for three 15-minute sessions each week. This instruction occurred outside the general education classroom during the 90-minute core reading block. The paraprofessional implemented a program that was focused on a whole-word, visual discrimination approach to reading. The special education teacher had most recently assessed Millie's reading skills at the beginning of third grade. Millie was able to read 21 sight words, including *my, the, yellow,* and *is.* She knew the names of 20 letters but could only produce the sound for *m.* On a kindergarten CBM of first-sound fluency, she was able to earn 6 points by providing correct first sounds (e.g., /Kă/ in *cat* for 1 point, /d/ in *dog* for 2 points) in 1 minute, a score well below the middle-of-year kindergarten benchmark score of 30 sounds in a minute. She was able to provide one correct letter sound in a minute on a CBM of letter–sound fluency, also well below the end-of-year kindergarten benchmark of 30 correct sounds in a minute. These data indicated a weakness in Millie's reading abilities and inadequate growth in reading skills across years.

Ms. Purser, in her second year of teaching at Hawkins Elementary, shared Ms. Ryder's concerns about Millie's limited reading progress. In the IEP team meeting, she suggested that Millie could benefit from receiving a phonics-based reading intervention delivered within the DBI framework. After some discussion, all members of the IEP team agreed with the plan to adjust Millie's reading instruction. The team decided that Millie would receive 45 minutes per day of one-on-one reading instruction in Ms. Purser's room. Ms. Purser would be the interventionist for 2 days each week; Mr. Schnapp, an experienced paraprofessional, would provide the intervention the remaining 3 days. The team decided that Mr. Schnapp would provide support for Millie during her inclusion in a portion of the third-grade 90-minute reading block, and this supplemental reading instruction would take place during the remainder of the time. The team wrote two new IEP goals for Millie to reflect this change of instructional focus:

- By the end of the school year, when presented with a first-sound fluency CBM probe, Millie will say 30 correct first sounds within 1 minute (middle-of-year kindergarten benchmark).
- By the end of the school year, when presented with a letter–sound fluency CBM probe, Millie will say 30 correct letter sounds within 1 minute (end-of-year kindergarten benchmark).

The team members decided they would begin Millie's new plan in 2 weeks, a sufficient amount of time for Ms. Purser to get everything ready. As the meeting closed, Dr. Dyer, the principal, expressed how impressed she was with the research and planning done by Ms. Ryder and Ms. Purser. The team members departed, optimistic for the next steps.

Special education teachers can implement the DBI framework on their own, or, as in our vignette, with team members. Although it is not required that the process be discussed at an IEP meeting, doing so increases the likelihood that multiple people will contribute to and support the process. For students with IDD, adapting instruction in a way that meets academic and behavioral needs often requires input from numerous professionals (e.g., speech–language pathologist, occupational therapist, behavior specialist). IEP meetings are some of the few times that all of these professionals are together to co-plan interventions, which is another reason to consider connecting the DBI process with the IEP. Furthermore, formalizing DBI implementation into a student's IEP increases the opportunity for family members (and students, when possible) to be involved in decision making and allows team members to make a plan for frequent communication about student progress. Initial discussions about implementing DBI should include conversations about the resources (e.g., intervention materials, interventionist expertise, time) that are needed to support DBI implementation. See Peterson et al. (Chapter 1, this volume) for resource suggestions.

Beyond broader, systems-level considerations for DBI implementation, teachers must also consider the ways that their students' reading intervention program is rooted in evidence-based practices for effective instruction. Before teachers begin planning to implement DBI with students with IDD, it may be useful to devote time to reviewing principles of effective instruction. It is likely that whether you are a preservice or inservice teacher, you have been exposed to these principles during training. However, if you are like us, a bit of review is always helpful.

First, we recommend that educators review features of explicit instruction, namely, instruction that is "systematic, direct, engaging, and success oriented" (Archer & Hughes, 2011, p. vii). This effective and efficient method for teaching students with disabilities includes modeling, guided practice, and independent practice. Or, as Archer and Hughes (2011) refer to this sequence, "I do it. We do it. You do it" (p. viii). Smith, Sáez, and Doabler (2016) explain that explicit instruction can optimize working memory function by making the learning process more observable—this is essential when providing intervention to students with IDD. These authors explain that delivering explicit instruction entails (1) strategically selecting and sequencing examples of new skills, (2) providing clear teacher explanations and models, (3) carefully guiding practice opportunities, and (4) monitoring student responses and providing immediate feedback. If you would like to learn more, we encourage you read *Explicit Instruction: Effective and Efficient Teaching* by Archer and Hughes (see *www.explicitinstruction.org*). Additionally, you can find examples of how explicit instruction can be applied across different domains (i.e., working memory, mathematics, read-alouds, and technology-based gaming interventions) in the July–August 2016 issue of *Teaching Exceptional Children* (Vol. 48, Issue 6).

Second, it may be equally helpful for teachers to review principles of effective reading or math instruction before planning DBI. The Institute of Education Sciences (IES; Foorman et al., 2016) has provided four recommendations for teaching foundational reading skills:

- Teach students academic language skills, including the use of inferential and narrative language, and vocabulary knowledge.
- Develop awareness of the segments of sounds in speech and how they link to letters.
- Teach students to decode words, analyze word parts, and write and recognize words.
- Ensure that each student reads connected text every day to support reading accuracy, fluency, and comprehension. (p. 2)

Although these recommendations are not specific to students with IDD, they are well aligned with Browder et al.'s (2009) model of literacy instruction for this population. Additional suggestions for delivering evidence-based reading intervention to children and adolescents with IDD can be found in *Individualized Research-Based Reading Instruction for Students with Intellectual Disabilities: Success Stories* (Allor, Mathes, Jones, Champlin, & Cheatham, 2010) and *10 Research-Based Tips for Enhancing Literacy Instruction for Students with Intellectual Disability* (Lemons, Allor, Al Otaiba, & LeJeune, 2016).

In the area of math, similar resources exist. The IES (Gersten et al., 2009) provided eight recommendations for teaching mathematics to students within an RTI framework. Four of those recommendations relate to the content of mathematics instruction:

- Instructional materials for students receiving interventions should focus intensely on in-depth treatment of whole numbers in kindergarten through grade 5 and on rational numbers in grades 4–8.
- Interventions should include instruction on solving word problems that is based on common underlying structures.
- Intervention materials should include opportunities for students to work with visual representations of mathematical ideas, and interventionists should be proficient in the use of visual representations of mathematical ideas.
- Interventions at all grade levels should devote about 10 minutes in each session to building fluent retrieval of basic arithmetic facts. (pp. 11–12)

Similar to the IES reading recommendations, the math recommendations are not specific to students with IDD; however, they are well aligned with Saunders, Bethune, Spooner, and Browder's (2013) recommendations for teaching mathematics standards to students with moderate and severe disabilities. Additionally, these authors recommend teachers of students with IDD incorporate evidence-based behavioral practices such as a constant time delay, least intrusive prompting, and task analysis to break down challenging mathematics procedures into manageable chunks and maximize student success. Three other useful resources further describe effective mathematics instruction and provide (1) overarching guidelines for delivering mathematics interventions to students with mathematics difficulties (Doabler et al., 2012), (2) an example of implementing DBI within mathematics instruction (Powell & Stecker, 2014), and (3) an applied model of how to plan effective, intensive mathematics instruction for students with IDD (Rivera & Baker, 2013).

When students' intervention plans begin with a program aligned to practices of effective instruction, teachers create a strong foundation to support students' growth without further adaptations. In this way, teachers can more confidently equate inadequate student progress with a need for more intensified, individualized instruction rather than a need for a missing core effective instructional practice.

Getting Started with DBI: Training

Ms. Purser's first step in implementing DBI with Millie was to learn more about the steps involved in DBI. She located two training modules from the IRIS Center, funded by the U.S. Office of Special Education Programs (OSEP). After completing the two modules during two planning periods, she had a clear understanding of how she was going to proceed with intensifying Millie's reading intervention and how she would collect data to guide her decision making. The second step was for Ms. Purser to verify that both she and Mr. Schnapp would be able to deliver the new reading intervention with fidelity. She selected Early Interventions in Reading (EIR) Level K as the intervention, because it is supported by research and is well aligned with Millie's IEP goals.

She scheduled a meeting with another teacher in the school who was currently using EIR. They discussed the program, and Ms. Purser studied the teacher's guide. She also observed two intervention groups participating in the intervention.

DBI Training

Educators who will be involved with DBI implementation likely need additional professional development. Minimally, the individuals who will be designing, delivering, and making adaptations to students' DBI plans need to understand each of the steps in the process. These are covered by Peterson et al. (Chapter 1, this volume). As many special education teachers already implement an informal process of making changes to instruction based on student response, the information covered in that chapter may be all that is needed for them to adapt their process to meet the systematic guidelines for DBI. There are several resources, outlined in that chapter, available for extended learning opportunities around DBI.

Intervention Training

It is also essential that interventionists involved in DBI implementation understand how to deliver the intervention they use. For experienced interventionists, reviewing the manuals that come with the intervention may be sufficient. For interventionists with less experience, participating in formal training from a certified trainer or in less formal training from a colleague who is familiar with the intervention may be valuable. In our experience, taking advantage of opportunities to observe another person delivering the intervention can be beneficial. Prior to implementing the intervention lessons with students, it is also helpful to allocate time for practicing the intervention steps. This provides an opportunity to preemptively identify the steps of the lesson that require more careful planning and material organization. These trial runs contribute to the smoothness of implementation when it matters most—during instruction with students.

Fidelity of Implementation

A final step of planning is to determine how interventionists will monitor fidelity of implementation (i.e., adherence to the plan) and track consistency of delivery (i.e., dosage). It is important to monitor the fidelity of both the intervention program and the implementation of the DBI process. At minimum, an interventionist who is implementing DBI independently should (1) develop a reflection checklist in which he or she could report on intervention delivery and note areas for which he or she will review guidance from the teacher's manual, and (2) keep a calendar or graph in which he or she reports dates and duration of intervention delivery and students' absences. This information would allow the interventionist (and his or her team if they are involved) to evaluate whether poor response may be due to less than optimal implementation or whether a student's nonresponse is caused by other factors that could indicate a need for adjustments. See Peterson et al. (Chapter 1, this volume) for resources to support fidelity of implementation.

DBI Step 1: Validated Intervention Program

Feeling confident that she understood how to deliver the intervention within a DBI framework, Ms. Purser knew that her next task was to ensure that the intervention would be delivered with sufficient intensity. After evaluating Millie's new plan, she confirmed that the change in intervention addressed many dimensions of intensification (e.g., strength, dosage, alignment, and comprehensiveness). EIR is a reading intervention program that has "strength," in that previous research demonstrated that students like Millie who received the program performed, on average, much better than similar students in a control condition (effect size = 0.69) on a standardized reading comprehension assessment (Allor et al., 2014). Ms. Purser's plan also satisfied the "dosage" dimension, because the plan included a substantial increase in reading intervention time (e.g., 45 minutes/day, 5 days/week vs. 15 minutes/day, 3 days/week). In addition, the new plan addressed "alignment," because the program addresses Millie's specific learning needs (i.e., alphabetic principle, decoding) and "comprehensiveness," in that EIR is an explicit instruction program targeting several key areas of early reading. With evidence that Millie's instructional plan was sufficiently intensive across dimensions, Ms. Purser completed preparation by training Mr. Schnapp to implement the intervention.

DBI implementation guidance recommends that interventionists start the process with a validated intervention program (also referred to as a *standard protocol* or *evidence-based intervention program*) when possible. Starting with an extant curriculum that experimental research has shown to improve student outcomes increases the likelihood that the student participating in DBI will respond favorably to the intervention plan. For teachers of students with IDD, it may be somewhat more challenging to identify a validated intervention program. In our example, Ms. Ryder selected EIR (Allor & Mathes, 2012), which has been validated by experimental research (Allor et al., 2014) to be effective for students like Millie—students with IDD.

Another resource for identifying validated intervention programs is the Tools Chart published by the National Center on Intensive Intervention (NCII; *www.intensiveintervention.org/chart/instructional-intervention-tools*). Although many of the programs have not been validated for use with students with IDD, many are closely aligned with recommendations for intervention in reading and math. In lieu of having additional research programs validated for students with IDD, these programs are possible starting points. To individualize intervention programs that have been validated more broadly for students with reading or math difficulties, it is helpful to consider resources that provide guidance on effective instructional practices specific to students with IDD (described earlier in this chapter). These practices can be layered onto a standard, evidence-based protocol to maximize alignment of your core intervention program to your students' needs. Building interventions in this way, you can craft an intervention package that pulls from overarching guidance for teaching students with IDD, despite the small evidence base for standard protocol intervention programs for this population.

After selecting a validated intervention program, the interventionist's next task is to consider whether any additional adaptations may be needed to establish that the planned intervention is sufficiently more intensive than previously attempted remediation efforts. In Millie's case, both Ms. Ryder and Ms. Purser expressed concern for Millie's lack of growth in her current reading intervention program. Ms. Ryder worked to make Millie's new intervention plan more intensive than previous remediation efforts by switching to EIR and increasing the frequency and duration of the intervention sessions.

As described by Peterson et al. (Chapter 1, this volume), Fuchs et al. (2017) recently published a taxonomy of intervention intensity that can guide interventionists as they evaluate interventions. In evaluating the intensity of an intervention, Fuchs et al. recommend that teachers consider seven dimensions. See Table 4.1 for an overview of these seven dimensions and relevant guiding questions to consider when evaluating and applying each dimension for students with IDD.

Finally, after the validated intervention program has been selected and the taxonomy of intervention intensity has been considered, we think it is critical to make sure the intervention plan is written down with sufficient detail. The NCII has developed various tools to support intensive intervention (*www.intensiveintervention.org/ tools-support-intensive-intervention-data-meetings*), including documents that can support the referral process, initial meetings about students' needs and the development of an intensive intervention plan, and ongoing meetings to monitor student progress. While it is not essential to use these specific forms, it is necessary to confirm that those involved with DBI implementation have a clear understanding of the intervention plan (i.e., curriculum to be used, adaptations for initial intensification, person responsible for delivery, intervention group size, intervention frequency and duration, progress monitoring plan, schedule for reviewing progress) and that this plan is documented and shared.

DBI Step 2: Progress Monitoring

Ms. Purser's final step was to determine how she was going to monitor Millie's progress. Ms. Purser decided that she would use the CBM progress monitoring measures aligned with Millie's IEP goals (i.e., first-sound fluency, letter–sound fluency) and the assessments included in EIR to guide her adaptation efforts. She decided she would administer the CBM probes every fourth week. For each measure, she planned on administering three probes and using Millie's median score for progress monitoring. She created a progress monitoring graph with aimlines for each of the measures. She constructed these aimlines by starting at Millie's current performance on each assessment (i.e., August 23 on Figure 4.1) and, counting ahead the instructional weeks until the end of the school year, marking Millie's IEP target goal for each measure (e.g., 30 correct sounds on the first-sound fluency measure by the end of the year). The EIR assessments are administered after every 20 lessons. Ms. Purser decided to schedule these at the same time as the CBM probes (see Figure 4.2). She set Millie's goal at 95% or greater for each assessment, as this would indicate mastery of a sufficient amount of the taught curriculum. She also decided that if Millie demonstrated less than 95% on the assessments, she would review lessons in that portion of the scope-and-sequence (e.g., Lessons 1–20) and readminister the EIR assessment after a week or two of additional review.

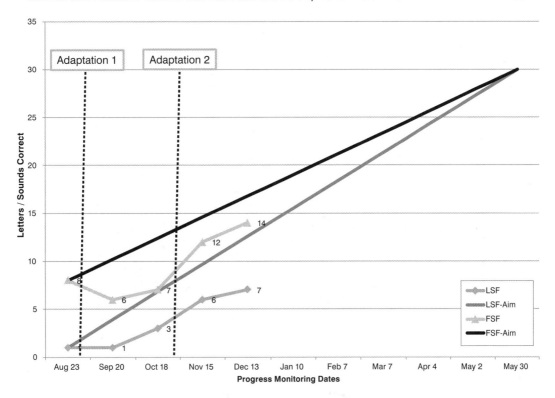

FIGURE 4.1. Millie's progress monitoring data. LSF, letter–sound fluency; FSF, first-sound fluency; Aim, aimline.

Ms. Purser decided that she would make adaptations to Millie's intervention if there were two consecutive data points below Millie's aimline on either of the CBM graphs. She thought this would be more appropriate for Millie since her data would be collected once every 4 weeks instead of weekly. She planned on using EIR assessment data to supplement her decision making and to help her evaluate whether Millie needed to repeat lessons. Ms. Purser also decided that she would closely monitor Millie's engagement during instruction and that she would be flexible with minor behavioral adaptations as needed.

The DBI process requires educators to collect frequent data to evaluate student response. Guidance for most students suggest that teachers should administer weekly CBM probes and make instructional adaptations if a student has four consecutive data points below his or her aimline (National Center on Intensive Intervention, 2013). Teachers of students with IDD are also encouraged to closely monitor student response; however, there are a few important points to consider with this population of learners.

Academic growth will likely occur at a slower rate for students with IDD compared with other learners. For example, Allor and colleagues (2014) demonstrated that many students with IDD who participated in their research study needed as many as 2–4

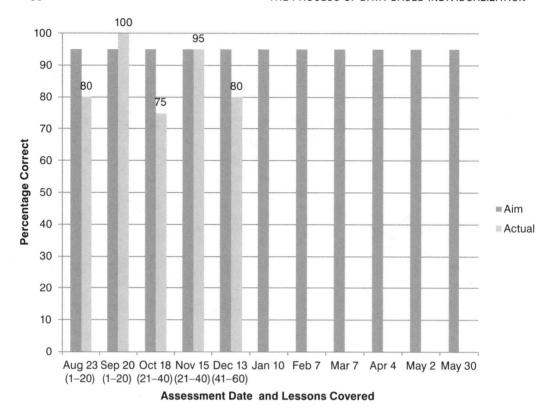

FIGURE 4.2. Millie's EIR assessment data. Aim, aimline.

academic years of intensive intervention to make 1 year's worth of academic progress. This finding suggests that students with IDD can achieve growth on generalized academic skills, as measured by CBMs, but that these learners often require a much longer duration of intervention. The longer duration often coincides with many more cycles of skills review before content mastery is demonstrated on general outcome measures such as CBMs.

As CBM may not be sensitive to shorter-term growth of students with IDD, we recommend that teachers supplement data collection by using measures that are more closely aligned with intervention. For example, teachers may follow Ms. Purser's model and administer assessments that are included in the validated intervention program. Although these measures likely have less information to support their technical adequacy, we believe they can still be useful to guide low-stakes instructional decisions. Additionally, teachers may want to collect data on targeted items that students are mastering. For example, in our reading intervention research, we often focus on a limited number of instructional targets (e.g., 3 letter sounds) at a time and assess each one on a daily basis (see Lemons, Mrachko, Kostewicz, & Paterra, 2012). When students have demonstrated the ability to correctly identify an instructional target for 3 consecutive days, we consider the item mastered and move on through the instructional scope and sequence. This type of intervention-aligned, proximal assessment of student learning can be more sensitive to student growth than other, more distal measures. Finally, teachers should also integrate informal assessments, including observations, analysis of student work, and data on behavior (e.g., on-task, engagement) to inform decisions on instructional adaptations.

In general, for teachers of students with IDD, we recommend following guidance on progress monitoring with some flexibility. It is likely that additional data sources beyond one or two CBMs will be necessary to guide decision making and that this step in the process will need to be implemented according to professional experience. In Millie's case, Ms. Purser collected data prior to the beginning of intervention and again 4–8 weeks later. Therefore, by the eighth week of intervention, the progress monitoring graphs provided the necessary evidence of adequacy of treatment response across measures.

DBI Steps 3, 4, and 5: Diagnostic Assessment, Intervention Adaptation, and Continued Progress Monitoring

Ms. Purser and Mr. Schnapp started the DBI plan with Millie on August 23rd. However, after only 2 weeks, both were concerned about off-task behaviors Millie was exhibiting during instruction. Millie often asked questions not related to the lesson and put her head down when either interventionist redirected her to the task. Ms. Purser reached out to Mr. McLaughlin, the behavior specialist on Millie's IEP team, and he agreed to observe one of her sessions that week. During his observation, Mr. McLaughlin collected data on Millie's off-task behavior by dividing the 45-minute session into 30-second intervals and recording whether Millie was off-task at the end of each interval (i.e., momentary time sampling; for an explanation, see Kuchle & Riley-Tillman, Chapter 3, this volume). Based on the data he collected, Mr. McLaughlin estimated that Millie was off-task for 75% of the lesson.

Mr. McLaughlin helped Ms. Purser design a visual schedule that included a picture and label for each activity in the lesson (e.g., first-sound pictures, oral blending) and a visual to indicate a break following lesson completion. They decided that the interventionist would help Millie draw a checkmark after completing each step, and then she could immediately have a short (i.e., 1- to 2-minute) break. After the short break, the interventionist would help her count how many more steps were required before the end of the lesson, when she could take a longer (i.e., 5- to 10-minute) break with her favorite toys. After making the initial behavioral adaptation, both Mr. Schnapp and Ms. Purser anecdotally noted a change in Millie's behaviors during intervention sessions. She exhibited fewer problem behaviors during the aspects of intervention with the greatest difficulty.

Ms. Purser and Mr. Schnapp continued following Millie's intervention and progress monitoring plan. After 8 weeks (see October 18th on Figures 4.1 and 4.2), the DBI team, including Ms. Ryder, met to discuss Millie's progress. During this meeting, Ms. Purser presented the EIR data to the team. Millie had required additional review of lessons, as she had not earned a score of 95% or greater on several of the EIR assessments.

However, at the most recent probe, Millie scored 100% on the assessment for Lessons 21–40. Millie's data on both CBMs demonstrated 2 weeks of consecutive performance below her aimlines. Ms. Purser noted that Millie often exhibited frustration when confronted with the letter–sound fluency student probe, which contained many letters not yet targeted during intervention. Millie typically responded in one of two ways: (1) overgeneralizing and stating the letter sounds she had mastered, regardless of the presented letter on the page, or (2) responding, "I don't know" to all letter sounds, including those with demonstrated mastery in the EIR context. On the first-sound fluency probe, Millie's score had decreased slightly, from 8 to 7 points per minute. Millie's data were far below her aimline.

The team decided to make two adaptations to Millie's intervention plan. First, the team noted that the EIR intervention was not introducing letter sounds very quickly. Ms. Purser decided that she would supplement the intervention by more quickly introducing the sounds of taught letters. Second, the team wanted to supplement Millie's phonological awareness development. A supplemental phonological awareness game called Stop and Go is available from the publishers of EIR. The game targets blending and segmenting of sounds, and it has been demonstrated through experimental research to enhance students' phonological awareness skills (Allor, Gansle, & Denny, 2006). The team decided that Mr. Schnapp would play the game with Millie and a classmate during her inclusion time twice per week, and Ms. Purser would incorporate the game into her intervention time once per week. Ms. Purser also agreed to provide Ms. Ryder with some review games that she could play with Millie at home. The team members wrote down their adaptations to the intervention plan and the interventionists made a plan to review the new steps. The team members left the meeting, confident that the adaptations would be helpful for Millie.

The iterative, ongoing cycle of intervention–assessment–adaptation is the critical element in the DBI process. Teachers should plan when adaptations will be made and determine on which data these decisions will be based before DBI implementation begins. However, as demonstrated in our vignette, we also think that there should be some flexibility in the implementation of adaptations for students with IDD. For many students with IDD, a substantially longer period of intervention may be needed before there is measurable change on progress monitoring measures. We encourage special educators to stick with the intervention plan and to implement minor adjustments before more major adaptations are made. Small adjustments to the plan that improve student behavior or engagement (based on informal, professional judgment) may occur more frequently and should be allowed before 6–8 weeks of intervention have occurred. In contrast, we recommend that more major changes, like changing the focus of instruction or the intervention materials to be used, be delayed until at least 6–8 weeks of intervention have occurred. Furthermore, we caution special educators against changing intervention *goals* based on poor student response. While this may be needed in rare circumstances, it is most likely that positive student change will occur if special educators use the DBI process to enhance instruction instead of reconsidering the goals that teachers and family members want students to achieve.

SUMMARY

Our purpose in this chapter has been to describe how one form of intensive intervention, DBI, can be integrated into the special education services provided to students with IDD. We have highlighted a few areas in which special considerations may be needed to adapt DBI guidance for students with IDD. We then described an example of Millie, and the process that her mother and teachers went through as they explored DBI implementation. We hope that you were able to see that DBI is a highly appropriate process to improve academic outcomes for students with IDD. We believe that if many of you who are reading this chapter attempt to integrate DBI into the special education services you provide, children and adolescents with IDD will continue to impress everyone with just how much they can accomplish.

APPLICATION EXERCISE 4.1

For our first application exercise, we would like you to evaluate what decisions you would make if you were Millie's special educator. Look at Figures 4.1 and 4.2. Consider that it is now December and you have two additional progress monitoring data points for Millie. Although her data are improving, she is still below her aimline on both CBMs. Additionally, she did not demonstrate mastery of 95% of skills on the EIR assessment.

On the letter–sound fluency measure, Millie earned a score of 7 letter sounds correct in a minute; her aimline goal was 13. She was able to provide the correct sounds for *a, t, m, f, s, c,* and *l*.

On the first-sound fluency measure, she earned a score of 14 points (aimline goal of 17). She was able to earn 2 points by providing the first phoneme in the words *nap, pots, pill, pants,* and *ran*. She earned 1 point by providing the first sound that included more than one phoneme by saying /br/ for *break,* /sp/ for *spend,* /kl/ for *clay,* and /sw/ for *swing*. She provided no correct sounds for *claws* and *shark*.

On the EIR assessment, she missed 7 of 35 items. She knew all of the four picture names; she was able to blend /mm/–/ooo/ into *moo* but was unable to blend the sounds of *sock, sea,* and *net*. She also stretched the word *moo* into /mmm/–/ooo/, but she could only say the first sound in *sea, net,* and *sock*. She named all of the letters that were assessed (i.e., *e, a, I, E, h, n, M, C, N, R, l, f, H, L,* and *i*). She also said the correct sounds for *T, t, M, f, a, A,* and *m*. She missed the sound for *F*.

Mr. Schnapp reports that Millie gets very distracted and off-task after 20 minutes of intervention. Ms. Purser feels that 45 minutes of one-on-one instruction may not be providing Millie with sufficient peer models.

Based on this information, what would you recommend in terms of making an adaptation to Millie's plan? Consider the data, the taxonomy of intervention intensity (Table 4.1), and your professional judgment of what steps may be needed to increase the intervention's ability to meet Millie's needs.

APPLICATION EXERCISE 4.2

For our second application activity, we want you to think about a child or adolescent with IDD that you know. Consider her or his current levels of performance and intervention needs. Next, use this chapter to work through planning each stage of DBI with this student. Consider locating the Fuchs et al. (2017) article to guide your planning of adaptations. It may be useful for you to download the planning documents from NCII to organize your plans (*https://intensiveintervention.org/implementation-support/tools-support-intensive-intervention-data-meetings*). Plan at least three ways that you would initially adapt the validated intervention program. Also, identify at least two ways that you would monitor progress, including a plan for when you would make additional adaptations based on poor student response.

FREQUENTLY ASKED QUESTIONS

How do I know whether a student with IDD needs intensive intervention?

It is likely that *all* students with IDD would benefit from intensive intervention. If this does not seem feasible, we recommend initially implementing DBI with students who have demonstrated the poorest response to current remediation efforts, or with students whose current levels of performance are substantially below those of peers who also have disabilities. Special educators who gain experience with implementing DBI with a few students will find it easier to involve additional students in subsequent academic years.

What if I don't think my paraprofessional should be responsible for so much instruction?

We believe that the paraprofessional is one of the most underutilized resources in special education. With appropriate training, coaching, and supervision, these staff members can deliver high-quality, intensive intervention. It is important that the special educator be the person responsible for designing the intervention and that he or she frequently monitor whether the paraprofessional is delivering the intervention accurately, and whether the student is demonstrating adequate response. We consider the example in which Ms. Purser and Mr. Schnapp shared instructional responsibilities across the week to be one appropriate model for including a paraprofessional in intervention.

I'm not sure that CBM will be useful for my student with IDD. Should I still use it?

CBM is an assessment tool that has strong empirical support for helping teachers make better decisions about student instruction (Stecker, Fuchs, & Fuchs, 2005). However, the research base on using CBM with students with IDD is less broad. We recommend that special educators consider CBMs that are aligned with student's goals and include these as one part (but not the only part) of the progress monitoring system. As we noted, students may require multiple years of intervention to obtain early grade-level benchmarks. However, we think these measures are important to use for the following reasons: (1) They are designed to monitor response to intervention over time; (2) they are closely aligned with critical early academic skills; (3) they are efficient to administer; and (4) they are fairly easy to describe to parents and other school personnel.

How flexible should I be in applying the guidance on making adaptations based on progress monitoring data for a student with IDD?

This is a tricky one. Implementation of DBI should not be haphazard. However, the complex needs of many students with IDD, combined with the challenges of accurately assessing academic skills in a way that is sensitive to growth, means that we cannot insist on an incredibly rigid system of implementation. Thus, we suggest that special educators will need to review the guidance provided in this chapter and in the remainder of this book and use professional judgment to design a system that will work for themselves and their students. The most important things are to have high expectations, to use data to inform your decision making in a timely manner, and to adapt instruction when students are not responding. Some of the finer details may be less important. Let the data guide you.

I'm still unclear how DBI might work for a student with IDD in middle or high school. Can you provide an example?

As described by Browder et al. (2009) and Lemons at al. (2016), the emphasis of literacy instruction for students with IDD will likely shift from focusing on "learning how to read" to "functional reading skills" as students move into middle and secondary settings. This focus should be determined for individual students by the IEP team. Regardless of the focus of literacy instruction, the DBI process can still be followed. What might change is the content of the instruction and the data that is collected for progress monitoring, and likely the process would need to be applied with a little more flexibility.

Consider Gaten, a 20-year-old man with IDD. He is finishing his final year in high school and will be transitioning to a postsecondary program at a local university next year. He reads at a third-grade level. Gaten and his IEP team have decided that goals for this academic year include (1) increasing Gaten's ability to use text-to-speech technology to access text, (2) increasing his ability to read words that will be useful for navigating his new college campus, and (3) improving his texting ability so he can keep in contact with friends and family.

Gaten's teachers could follow the steps of DBI to help him achieve each of these goals. For example, the teacher could select a user-friendly text-to-speech app and conduct a task analysis to outline the steps Gaten would need to learn to use the app successfully. Then, the teacher could keep data on his learning of the steps and make adaptations to her instruction if Gaten is not making progress. Should she get stuck, she could collect diagnostic assessment data (e.g., observe Gaten using the app and identify errors, interview him about his app use) to guide adaptations to instruction. The iterative DBI process would help the teacher to frequently evaluate Gaten's progress and to make timely changes to instruction when needed.

ACKNOWLEDGMENTS

Development of this chapter was supported in part by Grants H325H140001 and H325D140073, both from the Office of Special Education Programs within the U.S. Department of Education. Nothing in the chapter necessarily reflects the positions or policies of the funding agencies and no official endorsement by them should be inferred.

REFERENCES

Allor, J. H., Gansle, K. A., & Denny, R. K. (2006). The stop and go phonemic awareness game: Providing modeling, practice, and feedback. *Preventing School Failure, 50*(4), 23–30.

Allor, J. H., & Mathes, P. G. (2012). *Early Interventions in Reading: Level K.* Bothell, WA: McGraw-Hill SRA.

Allor, J. H., Mathes, P. G., Jones, F. G., Champlin, T. M., & Cheatham, J. P. (2010). Individualized research-based reading instruction for students with intellectual disabilities: Success stories. *Teaching Exceptional Children, 42*(3), 6–12.

Allor, J. H., Mathes, P. G., Roberts, J. K., Cheatham, J. P., & Al Otaiba, S. (2014). Is scientifically based reading instruction effective for students with below-average IQs? *Exceptional Children, 80*(3), 287–306.

Archer, A. L., & Hughes, C. A. (2011). *Explicit instruction: Effective and efficient teaching.* New York: Guilford Press.

Browder, D. M., Gibbs, S., Ahlgrim-Delzell, L., Courtade, G. R., Mraz, M., & Flowers, C. (2009). Literacy for students with severe developmental disabilities: What should we teach and what should we hope to achieve? *Remedial and Special Education, 30*(5), 269–282.

Deno, S. L. (1985). Curriculum-based measurement: The emerging alternative. *Exceptional Children, 52,* 219–232.

Doabler, C. T., Cary, M. S., Jungjohann, K., Clarke, B., Fien, H., Baker, S., . . . Chard, D. (2012). Enhancing core mathematics instruction for students at risk for mathematics disabilities. *Teaching Exceptional Children, 44,* 48–57.

Endrew F. v. Douglas County School District, RE-1, 580 U.S. (2017).

Foorman, B., Beyler, N., Borradaile, K., Coyne, M., Denton, C. A., Dimino, J., . . . Wissel, S. (2016). *Foundational skills to support reading for understanding in kindergarten through 3rd grade* (NCEE 2016-4008). Washington, DC: National Center for Education Evaluation and Regional Assistance (NCEE), Institute of Education Sciences, U.S. Department of Education.

Fuchs, L. S., Fuchs, D., & Malone, A. S. (2017). The taxonomy of intervention intensity. *Teaching Exceptional Children, 50,* 35–43.

Gersten, R., Beckmann, S., Clarke, B., Foegen, A., Marsh, L., Star, J. R., & Witzel, B. (2009). *Assisting students struggling with mathematics: Response to intervention (RTI) for elementary and middle schools* (NCEE 2009-4060). Washington, DC: National Center for Education Evaluation and Regional Assistance, Institute of Education Sciences, U.S. Department of Education.

Lemons, C. J., Allor, J. H., Al Otaiba, S., & LeJeune, L. M. (2016). 10 research-based tips for enhancing literacy instruction for students with intellectual disability. *Teaching Exceptional Children, 49*(1), 18–30.

Lemons, C. J., Mrachko, A. A., Kostewicz, D. E., & Paterra, M. F. (2012). The effectiveness of phonological awareness and decoding interventions for children with Down syndrome: Three single-subject studies. *Exceptional Children, 79*(1), 67–90.

Lemons, C. J., Zigmond, N., Kloo, A., Hill, D. R., Mrachko, A. A., Paterra, M. F., . . . Davis, S. M.

(2013). Performance of students with significant disabilities on early grade curriculum-based measures of word and passage reading fluency. *Exceptional Children, 79*(4), 408–426.

National Center on Intensive Intervention. (2013). *Data-based individualization: A framework for intensive intervention.* Washington, DC: Office of Special Education, U.S. Department of Education.

Powell, S. R., & Stecker, P. M. (2014). Using data-based individualization to intensify mathematics intervention for students with disabilities. *Teaching Exceptional Children, 46,* 31–37.

Rivera, C. J., & Baker, J. N. (2013). Teaching students with intellectual disability to solve for x. *Teaching Exceptional Children, 46,* 14–21.

Saunders, A. F., Bethune, K. S., Spooner, F., & Browder, D. (2013). Solving the common core equation: Teaching mathematics CCSS to students with moderate and severe disabilities. *Teaching Exceptional Children, 45,* 24–33.

Smith, J. L. M., Sáez, L., & Doabler, C. T. (2016). Using explicit and systematic instruction to support working memory. *Teaching Exceptional Children, 48*(6), 275–281.

Stecker, P. M., Fuchs, L. S., & Fuchs, D. (2005). Using curriculum-based measurement to improve student achievement: Review of research. *Psychology in the Schools, 42*(8), 795–819.

Turnbull, H. R., Turnbull, A. P., & Cooper, D. H. (2018). The Supreme Court, *Endrew,* and the appropriate education of students with disabilities. *Exceptional Children, 84*(2), 124–140.

Wei, X., Blackorby, J., & Schiller, E. (2011). Growth in reading achievement of students with disabilities, ages 7 to 17. *Exceptional Children, 78*(1), 89–106.

PART II

IMPLEMENTATION OF DATA-BASED INDIVIDUALIZATION

CHAPTER 5

Why Is Implementation Readiness Critical?

SARAH V. ARDEN
JENNIFER D. PIERCE

GUIDING QUESTIONS

➤ What does readiness to implement intensive intervention look like?
➤ How can we assess level of readiness for implementation?
➤ How can we overcome barriers and build capacity for initial implementation?

Data-based individualization (DBI), described in detail in previous chapters in this book, is a framework for intensifying intervention in an iterative and systematic fashion. Research suggests that educators who implement DBI improve student achievement outcomes more than those who do not, especially when DBI is implemented as part of a multi-tiered systems of support (MTSS) framework (L. S. Fuchs & Fuchs, 1986; Fuchs, Fuchs, & Stecker, 2010; D. Fuchs, Fuchs, & Vaughn, 2014).

Implementing DBI is not easy, however. Implementation researchers studying DBI have identified a set of essential elements that must be in place in order for it to be successful. These elements include (1) leadership and staff commitment, (2) implementation teams dedicated to focusing on the DBI process, (3) progress monitoring, (4) data-informed intervention planning, and (5) access for students with disabilities (National Center on Intensive Intervention [NCII], 2013). If sites lack these elements, then it is an indication they may not be ready to implement DBI, and it is highly unlikely that they will see success in even the earliest implementation efforts.

As educators, we can have a tendency to jump "feet-first" into use of new programs and practices (often referred to as *innovations*; Cook & Odom, 2013), typically because we are energized by the allure of promised student improvement or because we have been mandated to implement something new for deserving students. This is often the case when it comes to practices that promise to increase outcomes for students with disabilities or for those students who have seemingly intractable learning needs.

In the rarest of cases, this "feet-first" approach to implementation may be effective for the short term: One teacher may initially implement the new practice, some students may show benefits, and the teacher may continue to use that practice over time (Fixsen, Naoom, Blase, & Friedman, 2005). However, when we aim to implement any educational innovation—especially one with multiple components, like DBI—*beyond* just one teacher, expect that innovation to sustain, *and* expect it lead to desired student outcomes, then we have to take different approach to *how* we engage our implementation efforts so that we do not end up getting stuck.

In short, for DBI to reach its full potential and achieve increased outcomes, we must take a strategic approach to implementation (Arden, Gandhi, Zumeta Edmonds, & Danielson, 2017; NCII, 2013) and consider not just *what* is implemented but also *how* it is implemented. This is because the work of implementing intensive intervention requires creative thinking and significant change in the way instruction and intervention are offered to students. And just as it would be ill-advised to suggest that an individual run a marathon without first assessing his or her readiness and capacity to do so, it is also unwise to suggest that educators implement DBI without doing the same. Without first attending to readiness for DBI, implementation is less prone to take hold for the long term (Bambara, Nonnemacher, & Kern, 2009). With these considerations in mind throughout this chapter, we follow the staff members at a fictitious school—Lincoln Elementary School—as they go through the process of determining their readiness to implement DBI. We learn what steps they took to assess readiness and to begin implementation.

INTRODUCTION TO LINCOLN ELEMENTARY

It is late spring and the staff and leadership of Lincoln Elementary School are beginning to think about creating class rosters for the following school year. To best support all teachers and students at Lincoln, staff members want to ensure that the classes they create are balanced with the right blend of students who are achieving at or above grade level and those who need additional support and intervention. Staff and leadership convene one afternoon during a staff meeting to review results from their universal screening assessment, which is administered in the fall, winter, and spring of each year. Upon close examination of the data, the staff members notice that students who scored at benchmark (i.e., at grade level) in the fall continued to score at or above that level throughout the year. They also notice that many students who scored in the fall at the targeted level, or just below grade level, demonstrated marked progress, either remaining close to grade level throughout the year or scoring at grade level by spring. The staff members were pleased with these data that showed progress for the majority of their students.

Unfortunately, when Lincoln staff members reviewed the data for students who scored far below grade level in the fall, they noticed less progress. Most students at this level remained below grade level throughout the year. Even more concerning, some students made very little progress at all throughout the year. These findings concerned the staff members at Lincoln Elementary, because they knew it was critically important that students with the most intensive needs achieve significant gains. They also knew that if they did not improve how they intervened with these students, students' learning needs would likely become more pronounced and challenging to address. When reflecting on their work with the students in this group, many of the staff members indicated that they felt particularly helpless, because none of the school's existing intervention programs seemed to work for these students.

Faced with this situation, the staff members at Lincoln began to research ways to support students with intensive needs. They quickly discovered DBI and decided they wanted to try it. However, once they set out to begin implementation, they quickly hit a roadblock. They had no idea what to do beyond making the initial decision to implement DBI. In fact, it seemed that deciding to implement the approach was the easiest part of the process! They wondered: How should we start? How can we build on what we are already doing that works well but change what does not? What do we need to take into consideration when asking staff to use DBI? Faced with these questions at this pressing roadblock, the staff members decided to learn more about implementation of DBI. And what was the key lesson they learned about moving the approach forward? Readiness.

READINESS AND THE "HOW": A STRATEGIC APPROACH TO IMPLEMENTATION

In the simplest sense, *readiness* is the degree to which the organization (i.e., the school, district, region, or even state) and the people working within it are primed to undertake the complex process of change (Fixsen, Blase, Horner, & Sugai, 2009; Pierce & Ruedel, submitted). Research suggests that two types of readiness—organizational readiness and innovation-related readiness—influence implementation outcomes (Damschroder et al., 2009). *Organizational readiness* refers to the necessary procedural components to support interventions, including the human, material, and, logistic mechanisms. *Innovation-related readiness* refers to the components of an innovation that are most difficult for educators to implement. With DBI, the word *innovation* is appropriate, because the term reflects the idea that some elements of DBI are novel, requiring educators to have expertise in specific aspects of the approach.

We suggest approaching readiness to implement DBI by sorting the essential elements descried earlier into these two categories of organizational readiness and innovation-related readiness (see Figure 5.1). For *organizational* readiness this includes leadership buy-in and staff commitment, intervention teams, and access for students with disabilities. For *innovation-related* readiness this includes data-informed intervention planning and use of progress monitoring data (see Figure 5.1). Categorizing readiness in this way allows implementers to consider both the infrastructure that needs to be developed and the knowledge and skills related to DBI that must also be in place. This categorization also allows implementers to see the intersections between the two categories and prioritize those areas (i.e., make sure there are committed staff members who have the knowledge to correctly use progress monitoring materials). In the following section, we review the key essential elements of DBI as they relate to organizational and innovation-related readiness and provide you with a few *critical questions* to ask yourself when considering your readiness to implement.

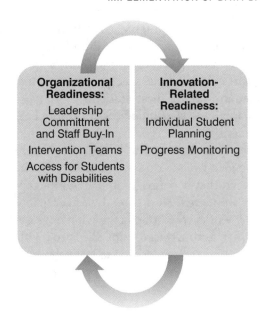

FIGURE 5.1. Key elements by readiness category.

Organizational Readiness

When we measure organizational readiness, we ask: What are the strengths of our organization that indicate we are ready to implement and utilize DBI? Do we have the right procedures (i.e., Tier 1 instruction, screening) already in place to support DBI? What barriers exist now that could halt initial *and* sustained implementation of intensive intervention (Arden et al., 2017; NCII, 2013). Understanding these strengths and barriers from the get-go allows us to build on what is working and to address obstacles that could hinder future implementation efforts. Moreover, by assessing organizational readiness we *initiate* implementation with clarity about the end goal; that is, we have clarity as to what sustained, effective implementation of intensive intervention should look like, and can clearly plan our steps to achieve our implementation goals. Gaining insight into this end goal from the first steps of implementation can propel continuous forward movement, especially in times when our typical practice changes (Fixen et al., 2009). The key elements of DBI that fall into the organizational readiness category are leadership buy-in and staff commitment, intervention teams, and a plan for ensuring access for students with disabilities.

Leadership and Staff Commitment

Readiness to implement DBI at the organizational level requires vocalized, explicit commitment from leaders such as the school principal and/or special education administrators *plus* the presence and commitment of a team that will be responsible for facilitating all implementation efforts. Explicit commitment from building leaders is especially important, as it sets the climate and culture in a school building and clearly lays out the priorities for the staff. Without leadership commitment, full DBI implementation

> **Critical Questions Related to Leadership and Staff Commitment**
>
> • What is our plan for getting feedback (e.g., implementation barriers, successes, needs, and questions) from stakeholders on DBI?
> • How will we ensure that we use this feedback to continuously improve the implementation of DBI?

rarely occurs (Arden et al., 2017). In addition to setting the climate and priorities, building leaders are able to ascertain whether the necessary resources (e.g., curricular and assessment materials, training and coaching, time, personnel) are available or can be allocated to support implementation of intensive intervention in the short *and* long term. Allocation of resources such as time and materials is critical to the success of DBI, as it helps bolster staff commitment and lessens the notion that by implementing DBI, staff members are being asked to engage "in one more thing" without additional support. Building (or district) leaders are also able to support organizational readiness by bolstering capacity to collect, analyze, and use data related to intensive intervention (e.g., student progress monitoring data, teacher fidelity data). One example of how this might happen is by ensuring that staff members have access to progress monitoring tools, providing professional development to use them, and establishing a climate in which data are prioritized.

In addition to considering leadership readiness and commitment, those implementing DBI should not forget other important stakeholders who are critical to the success of schoolwide practices including teachers, paraeducators, coaches, parents, and students (Fixsen et al., 2009; Pierce & Ruedel, submitted). Because implementation of DBI often asks practitioners to change the way they have traditionally delivered interventions, scheduled intervention time, and allocated human resources, it is important to consider how such changes will impact these stakeholders. Leaders should plan to ask them for their insight on a regular basis so they can begin to understand how DBI impacts them. Although it may seem obvious, asking stakeholders for their feedback *and* using that feedback to make improvements is a powerful strategy for building widespread buy-in (Damschroeder et al., 2009).

Implementation Teams

As we mentioned earlier, the implementation of DBI does not happen in isolation; it requires leadership, staff, and stakeholder commitment. And given that many schools have limited resources, it is crucial that educators band together to divvy up the responsibilities for implementing something as complex and resource laden as DBI. Additionally, research shows that sites that use teams to guide their readiness and initial implementation efforts can dramatically increase the speed at which implementation occurs (Fixsen, Blase, Timbers, & Wolf, 2001; Balas & Boren, 2000; Green & Seifert, 2005).

Think back to the five steps of the DBI process outlined by Peterson, Danielson, and Fuchs (Chapter 1, this volume). Part of that process tasks practitioners with engaging in sophisticated analysis of student-level data and collection of diagnostic data to inform

> **Critical Questions Related to Implementation Teams**
>
> - What teams are already in place on campus?
> - Do any of these teams already discuss students with intensive needs? Are there multiple teams that consist of the same, or similar, staff who discuss the same, or similar, students?
> - In order to implement DBI, do we need to develop a new team, or it is possible to repurpose existing teams?
> - Have we provided dedicated, regular planning times for teams to meet to discuss DBI?

intervention decisions. This is not a simple task! Engaging in the DBI process requires practitioners to make decisions about the science of intervention delivery and the art of individualization that are timely and grounded in data. In order for DBI to work, these kinds of decisions are best made in teams that consist of core members with regular times to meet and who follow a documented process. We have found that core members of a DBI intervention team must include leadership, special education staff, intervention staff, and general education representatives, and advise that other, related service delivery staff, parents, and even students themselves participate on an as-needed basis and/or when appropriate (NCII, 2013).

It is not uncommon to come across schools in which many teams that discuss student progress are already in place (i.e., grade level teams, data review teams, student study teams, problem-solving teams, MTSS-academic and MTSS-behavior teams). In fact, sometimes schools have so many teams that the role of each team has become unclear, as well as who is considered a critical member! When reflecting on readiness to implement DBI, we suggest thinking about how to streamline any redundancies in the teaming structure on campus and focus on identifying staff with the right expertise to participate in DBI.

Access for Students with Disabilities

There are a handful of characteristics that distinguish DBI (Danielson & Rosenquist, 2014) as a unique system for impacting student outcomes. One important factor to consider is the relationship between DBI and special education. Intensive intervention is intended for a small group of students for whom core instruction (i.e., Tier 1) and secondary intervention (i.e., Tier 2) have been insufficient to facilitate adequate progress. Students with disabilities often fall into this small group. Unfortunately, the reality in many schools is that students who have individualized education programs (IEPs) do not have access to intensive intervention (i.e., Tier 3 in an MTSS system) in their school buildings, because they receive services in special education instead, and schools are not always organized to coordinate supports across general and special education.

Although in some schools there are special education services available for providing students access to the most intensive and individualized supports, unfortunately, in other schools special education is actually *less* intensive and individualized than other

> **Critical Questions Related to Access for Students with Disabilities**
>
> - In what tier do students with disabilities receive the majority of their services?
> - Who delivers the instruction to students with disabilities?
> - Do these students have access to all tiers of instruction if needed?
> - Are students with disabilities making adequate progress toward their IEP goals and objectives?
> - What steps are taken if students with disabilities are not making progress?

supports offered within the same building (Arden et al., 2017). This weakening of special education services occurs for a host of reasons, but most commonly is the case when special education teachers are spread too thin and less skilled paraprofessionals are given the task of providing specialized instruction, and in places where inclusive settings are the only option for delivering specially designed instruction. Special education is weakened in places where schoolwide progress monitoring efforts stop for students once they receive special education and are instead replaced by processes to assess progress toward IEP goals and objectives that are not grounded in sound measurement methods. Whatever the reason, it is critical for the successful implementation of DBI that students with disabilities be included and have access to all tiers of intervention within a multitiered system, including intensive intervention. Not only does providing this access give educators a better shot at increasing outcomes for these students, researchers have found that sites that include students with disabilities experience stronger implementation, more meaningful data collection, increased collaboration, and increasingly inclusive cultures (Arden et al., 2017; Gandhi, Vaughn, Stelitano, Scala, & Danielson, 2015). For these reasons, access to all intervention tiers for students with disabilities is a clear sign of organizational readiness for DBI. When considering readiness for implementation of DBI, educators need to take a close look at special education practices in their buildings to ensure that students with disabilities are granted access to all ongoing interventions at the site.

Innovation-Related Readiness

Although organizational readiness is necessary, it is not sufficient; we also must explore *beyond* the logistical mechanisms in a school and ascertain the degree to which educators responsible for using DBI with students have the necessary knowledge and skills to do so. Because two of the most complex aspects of DBI include data-informed intervention planning and using progress monitoring data, we have found that innovation-related readiness is particularly important in these two key areas.

Data-Informed Intervention Planning

When implementing DBI, educators are asked to make individualized instructional decisions with a level of intensity and focus they may not have previously used. As

> ### Critical Questions Related to Data-Informed Intervention Planning
>
> - Do practitioners have access to professional learning opportunities that build their skills and knowledge of the intervention materials they need?
> - Is there a documented process on our site for tracking intervention decisions and following up on their success?
> - How have we provided support to staff, so that they are able to readily use the process?

we mentioned previously, DBI is not a one-time fix or scripted program; rather, it is an iterative process of intervention, progress monitoring, and adaptation over time. To add to the difficult nature of the work, students who are candidates for DBI have not historically responded to increasingly intensive intervention and require complex, individualized supports to access instruction that often go beyond adding more time or reducing the group size where intervention is delivered. Designing and delivering DBI is clearly complicated work for even the most experienced educators. We therefore want to know *before* we implement the degree to which teachers know how to engage in individualized intervention planning and delivery.

Collecting data about the knowledge and skills of the implementers (i.e., teachers, interventionists, paraprofessionals) can be used to provide a meaningful sequence of training and coaching for educators on data-informed intervention planning. After all, high-quality professional learning opportunities are an important piece in building educator knowledge and skill. To establish readiness among staff members to make individual student-level decisions, we suggest taking a quick inventory of the expertise on site, as well as engage in a process or protocol review for any existing intervention teams. In addition, we suggest that intervention teams focused on DBI follow a *consistent meeting process* that includes documentation of a brief overview of student progress, time to brainstorm individualized instructional adaptations based on the data, and assignment of responsible staff to deliver and track the success of the adaptations. Having a preestablished process for the meetings helps build the capacity of educators engaged in DBI by allowing them to focus on the nuances of providing data-informed intervention planning rather than shifting their attention to learning how to facilitate a meaningful meeting. Moreover, a clear and institutionalized meeting process enhances the chances that the intervention adaptations are actually made and allows teams to more quickly hone in on intensifications that are and are not working for individual students (for further discussion of effective meeting procedures, see Marx & Goodman, Chapter 6, this volume).

Progress Monitoring Data

As you learned from Pentimonti, Fuchs, and Gandhi (Chapter 2, this volume), assessments such as progress monitoring are at the heart of DBI. When collected and analyzed correctly (e.g., weekly), progress monitoring data provide us important information

> ### Critical Questions Related to Progress Monitoring Data
>
> - What are the right progress monitoring data to collect and what data are superfluous?
> - How can we help educators understand why these data are so powerful?
> - What types of decisions do educators make after collecting the data, and how often are those decisions made?

about incremental growth that is often made by struggling students with the most intensive academic and behavioral needs. Without these data, we lack a clear indication of the impact of our instruction and intensification and cannot make more sophisticated, timely, and individualized student-level decisions.

Unfortunately, many educators are unprepared to engage in the kind of systematic progress monitoring processes required to successfully implement DBI. For example, educators cite difficulties with adhering to a weekly data collection schedule, making sense of the data for timely intervention decisions, and understanding the value of progress monitoring data. Many educators even find the *idea* of progress monitoring data overwhelming (Roehig, Duggar, Moats, Glover, & Mincey, 2008), particularly when they are just beginning to use make sense of complicated screening data, including the use of decision rules for tier placement and tier movement. However, collecting and analyzing progress monitoring data is critical, and it is no small feat. It is often the case that once progress monitoring data are collected, many sites find themselves in a state of being *data rich and information poor* (D. Fuchs et al., 2014): without the sophisticated skills required to collect the right data and use it to make individualized, student-level decisions. For these reasons, we suggest that one additional aspect of innovation-related readiness involves educators' knowledge of and skill for using progress monitoring data. After ensuring that schools are using schoolwide screening appropriately (e.g., have decision rules in place for moving students into and out of tiers and rely on sound decision rules as way to identify the right students for DBI), it is important to *prepare* educators for successfully conducting progress monitoring and using the data for timely decision making.

MEASURING READINESS AND OVERCOMING BARRIERS

Now that we have discussed the critical questions that should be asked as we begin exploring readiness to implement DBI, we can move on to the actual work of measuring readiness. Readiness can be measured using a variety of tools. We suggest that sites review existing tools and customize them to fit their specific needs, contexts, and usage. For example, the NCII's DBI Fidelity Interview and Companion Rubric (NCII, 2015a, 2015b) guides users to focus on the implementation of intensive intervention, highlighting unique considerations related to intensive intervention rather than a broader response-to-intervention (RTI) framework. Organizations interested in pinpointing readiness for intensive intervention may find it beneficial to use this tool. Another tool to consider is the Center on Response to Intervention (CRTI) RTI Fidelity Rubric (CRTI, 2014a) and its companion Scoring Rubric (CRTI, 2014b) tool that can help guide self-assessment of readiness to implement RTI. These tools address the use of intensive intervention within the context of RTI and therefore contain information on core (i.e., Tier 1) instruction and assessment, strategic (i.e., Tier 2) intervention and assessment, and intensive intervention and assessment (i.e., Tier 3).

In addition to providing readiness interviews and rubrics, both the NCII and CRTI websites include self-paced training modules that cover topics such as preparing to implement RTI and readiness for DBI implementation, as well as handouts, facilitators' guides, and additional resources to support practitioners as they utilize these materials (see Table 5.1). Application Exercises 5.1 and 5.2 at the end of this chapter provide directions and guidance for sites hoping to utilize these materials to measure readiness.

TABLE 5.1. Resources for Measuring Readiness

Resource	Purpose	Location
Center on Response to Intervention (CRTI) Implementer Series	Provides foundational knowledge about essential components and implementation of RTI, specifically focused on planning for RTI and data-based individualization	*www.rti4success.org/video/planning-and-first-steps-rti*
CRTI Implementation Integrity Rubric	Supports monitoring of school-level fidelity of RTI implementation and can also be used as a readiness self-assessment	*www.rti4success.org/resource/essential-components-rti-integrity-rubric-and-worksheet*
National Center on Intensive Intervention (NCII) Data-Based Individualization (DBI) Readiness Module	Provides an overview readiness to implement DBI process and in-depth discussion on each critical component	*https://intensiveintervention.org/resource/getting-ready-implement-intensive-intervention-infrastructure-data-based-individualization*
NCII Fidelity Resources	Includes tools and resources related to monitoring the fidelity of implementation of intensive intervention	*www.intensiveintervention.org/fidelity-resources*
NCII Implementation Interview	Supports the monitoring of school-level implementation of DBI and also can be used as a readiness self-assessment	*www.intensiveintervention.org/resource/dbi-implementation-rubric-and-interview*

Note. Adapted from Arden, Gandhi, Zumeta Edmonds, and Danielson (2017). Reprinted with permission from SAGE Publications.

CHECKING IN ON LINCOLN

Think back to the work of Lincoln Elementary School early in its journey toward implementing DBI. As soon as the staff members made the decision to implement, they felt stuck. What should they do next? Who would be responsible for making sure implementation occurred, now and for the long term? How could they get ready for DBI?

When they began to feel stuck, the staff members at Lincoln decided to conduct additional research on DBI and they came across the NCII DBI Readiness Module and DBI Fidelity of Implementation Interview and Rubric. The principal assigned a small group of staff members that included special and general education representatives to read the module and come to a meeting prepared with questions. At the meeting, the team decided to use the DBI Fidelity of Implementation Interview to self-assess their readiness and to guide their next steps.

The team set aside a few hours during a planning meeting to review the interview and score their baseline readiness. Once the data were scored, Lincoln staff members reviewed their areas of strength and areas where they needed to grow. The data indicated that while staff members felt confident in their school's leadership commitment and buy-in, additional steps could be made by the principal to ensure that teachers received coaching on how to review student-level data during grade-level meetings. Additionally, the staff members at Lincoln realized that many general education teachers felt like they were lacking in the knowledge and skills required to provide small-group instruction within their classrooms and could benefit from some simple supports, such as a menu or checklist of options.

By assessing readiness, Lincoln staff members learned that many of the students with the most intensive needs (i.e., those who continually demonstrated limited progress) were receiving their instruction primarily in small groups run by paraprofessionals who had not been trained to use the curriculum to which they had access. One final, but crucial, piece of data revealed by the readiness interview was a lack of decision rules used by the staff at Lincoln. For example, staff did not know how many data points to collect before changing an intervention, and both general and special education teachers indicated they did not know what was required of them before referring students to receive additional intervention. Teachers also indicated they did not know how to adapt, or intensify, interventions without switching out programs entirely. This resulted in some teachers keeping students in Tier 2 instruction far longer than they should be and others referring students to Tier 3 before systematically implementing any interventions at all.

Using Readiness Data to Support Initial and Sustained Implementation

With readiness data on hand, the next step for Lincoln (or any site using this process!) is to use that information to drive implementation efforts forward. To be clear, *measuring* readiness may be the easy part; *analyzing* data such that clear conclusions are drawn, then *using* those data to drive implementation forward will likely be more difficult and take time (Gishar, Hilt-Panahan, Clements, & Shapiro, 2011). To ease the data analysis phase, it may be helpful to recognize that specific barriers often exist when implementing intensive intervention. For example, educators may not clearly understand how the use of intensive intervention "fits" into existing practices and may not agree that there is an urgent need for it; resources may not yet be allocated toward capacity-building opportunities (e.g., training and coaching); and existing policies may conflict with the use of intensive intervention.

Knowing about typical barriers during the data analysis phase may help alleviate worries that too many unsurmountable obstacles exist and that forward movement with intensive intervention is not possible. We suggest that once analysis of readiness occurs, sites make a strategic plan to leverage their strengths and prioritize addressing their areas of growth in a systematic fashion. For example, at Lincoln Elementary, both special education and general educators felt that they lacked examples of ways to intensify instruction. So the intervention team met and developed a menu of intensification practices, disseminated them at an all-staff-members meeting, and provided a brief training on their use and information about where teachers could learn more. By engaging in this small and easy step toward readiness, those practitioners implementing DBI felt like they had made progress tackling their school needs and did not require systematic reorganization of schoolwide practices. The staff at Lincoln decided to address the issue of intervention delivery by paraprofessionals *after* their staff members reported feeling more comfortable using the intensification menu. This shift would require a much more exhaustive overhaul of the way intervention was delivered on campus. Completing the readiness self-assessment and prioritizing this way allowed the Lincoln staff members to approach implementation strategically, armed with the knowledge they needed to understand the key elements of DBI and the critical questions to examine along the way.

SUMMARY

Implementing a system of intensive intervention is no easy task. It challenges status quo thinking and business-as-usual processes in many schools. DBI is a research-based mechanism for doing just that. Measuring readiness to implement DBI can help ease the unwieldy and cumbersome parts of implementation and can guide educators to strategically plan to leverage strengths and overcome barriers as implementation begins, and it is, arguably, one of the most critical parts of the implementation process. Remember that while we suggest that implementation of DBI occur at the schoolwide level, the tenets of DBI can always be implemented within one classroom or a team of classrooms. Regardless, assessing readiness to implement (whether at the schoolwide or classroom level) is a critical part of the DBI process and should not be overlooked. By attending to readiness, school teams can collect baseline data and approach implementation in a strategic way that allows educators to successfully build complex systems and work toward sustainability.

APPLICATION EXERCISE 5.1. Readiness Module and Planning

1. Think about the school where you currently work or one where you worked previously.

2. Using that site as a model, imagine a team of administrators, special and general education staff members who are responsible for leading the implementation of DBI.

3. Review readiness module on NCII website: *https://intensiveintervention.org/resource/getting-ready-implement-intensive-intervention-infrastructure-data-based-individualization.*

4. Answer the DBI Planning Guide Questions below and rate the school's and/or team's readiness to implement on a scale of 1–5.

   a. What are your long-term goals for implementing intensive intervention? (List up to three.)

   b. Are you currently implementing a tiered system of support (e.g., MTSS, RTI, PBIS)? If so, how might intensive intervention fit into your school or district's existing structure?

   c. What do you consider essential elements for successful implementation?

   d. Thinking about what you have learned in the module, rate your district's readiness for intensive intervention (on a scale of 1–5, with 5 indicating strong readiness).

5. Complete the action planning table (see Figure 5.2) and determine next steps: For this section, Goals should be measurable objectives you expect to be able to achieve by the end of the school year. Strategies and Action Items are concrete steps that help you achieve each goal.

Goal	Strategy/action items	Planning/supports/ resources needed	Timeline	Responsible staff

FIGURE 5.2. Action planning table.

APPLICATION EXERCISE 5.2. Baseline Capacity Interview

1. Convene a team comprised of administrators, special education, and general education staff who are responsible for leading the implementation of DBI.

2. Visit the NCII website and download copies of the DBI Implementation Interview and Rubric (*www.intensiveintervention.org/resource/dbi-implementation-rubric-and-interview*).

3. Block off a period of 2–3 hours in which the team members can meet to complete a self-assessment of their readiness to implement DBI.

4. Review each section of the interview and rubric and collectively rate your readiness to implement across each category. Please remember that this activity is intended to measure your *baseline readiness* so you should expect that you will not earn a high initial score in many categories.

5. Review your scores as a team and collectively prioritize which elements you need to tackle first (e.g., put in place progress monitoring measures, bolster accessibility of intervention curriculum) to be ready to implement DBI.

FREQUENTLY ASKED QUESTIONS

How do I know if my school (district) is ready to implement DBI? What can I do to get ready for implementation?

We suggest you review the NCII DBI Fidelity of Implementation Tool to learn about the essential elements of DBI that need to be in place before implementation occurs. Application Exercise 5.1 provides step-by-step suggestions for assessing baseline levels of readiness and ideas for putting the essential elements of DBI in place prior to implementation.

What do I do if my principal doesn't support schoolwide implementation of DBI?

While schoolwide implementation of DBI is ideal for the success of the framework, the process of data-based decision making can be implemented at a variety of levels including within grade-level teams or within one classroom. A teacher can employ many of the strategies within DBI (e.g., progress monitoring, collecting diagnostic data, intensifying and adapting intervention) in their own classroom. Implementing DBI at the classroom level can be especially beneficial for special education teachers as they track progress on students' IEP goals and objectives.

I've measured our baseline readiness to implement. Now what?

Once you have measured baseline readiness to implement, we suggest you prioritize your next steps in a strategic, sequential way, based on your site's capacity. For example, if you your site does not have a process for progress monitoring in place, then this might be a good place to begin. Building and sustaining complex systems is challenging work, and we suggest taking steps one at a time to help ensure smooth implementation.

Do I need special education and general education staff to be on board before I implement?

It is always ideal to have special education and general education staff on board before implementation begins. We understand, however, that this is not always the case in every school. However, staff members' buy-in and commitment to the process are directly related to implementation success, so while DBI can be implemented without having every staff member on board, we suggest trying to bridge the general-to-special education gap, if at all possible.

I work in a middle school or a high school. Can I implement DBI, and does assessing readiness differ at this level?

Yes! DBI can be implemented at both the middle school and high school level. However, just as in elementary schools, assessing readiness is critical for successful implementation at the middle and high school level and requires careful consideration of a number of factors that differ from elementary schools including (but not limited to) addressing credit accrual, meeting graduation requirements for students far below grade level, accessing evidence-based practices for students in older grades, and supporting content teachers (e.g., science, history, government) as they work with students who struggle to read. For additional guidance, we suggest you review the CRTI website focused on considerations for secondary school (*www.rti4success.org/related-rti-topics/secondary-schools*).

What is the best way to communicate to parents and families about DBI?

Parents and families are critical stakeholders in the DBI process, and we always suggest that they be involved. If students with disabilities are involved in the DBI process, one way to communicate with families and parents is through progress reporting on IEP goals and objectives. In addition, we suggest sharing progress monitoring graphs, goal-setting documents, and other relevant information using jargon-free, family-friendly language that clearly explains the interventions and progress monitoring data. It is also critical to communicate if out-of-grade-level monitoring occurs as part of the process, so every stakeholder is on the same page!

REFERENCES

Arden, S. V., Gandhi, A., Zumeta Edmonds, R., & Danielson, L. (2017). Toward more effective systems: Lessons from national implementation efforts. *Exceptional Children, 83*(3), 269–280.

Balas, E. A., & Boren, S. A. (2000). Managing clinical knowledge for health care improvement. In J. Bemmel & A. T. McCray (Eds.), *Yearbook of medical informatics 2000* (pp. 65–70). Columbia: University of Missouri.

Bambara, L. M., Nonnemacher, S., & Kern, L. (2009). Sustaining school-based individualized positive behavior support: Perceived barriers and enablers. *Journal of Positive Behavior Interventions, 11*(3), 161–176.

Center on Response to Intervention. (2012). *RTI Implementer Series: Module 1. Screening.* Washington, DC: U.S. Department of Education, Office of Special Education Programs, Center on Response to Intervention.

Center on Response to Intervention. (2014a). *RTI Fidelity of Implementation Rubric.* Washington, DC: U.S. Department of Education, Office of Special Education Programs, Center on Response to Intervention. Retrieved March 3, 2018, from *https://rti4success.org/sites/default/files/rti_fidelity_rubric.pdf.*

Center on Response to Intervention. (2014b). *RTI Essential Components Integrity Worksheet.* Washington, DC: U.S. Department of Education, Office of Special Education Programs, Center on Response to Intervention. Retrieved March 3, 2018, from *https://rti4success.org/sites/default/files/rti_fidelity_rubric_worksheet.pdf.*

Cook, B. G., & Odom, S. L. (2013). Evidence-based practices and implementation science in special education. *Exceptional Children, 79*(2), 135–144.

Damschroder, L. J., Aron, D. C., Keith, R. E., Kirsh, S. R., Alexander, J. A., & Lowery, J. C. (2009). Fostering implementation of health services research findings into practice: A consolidated framework for advancing implementation science. *Implementation Science, 4*(1), 50.

Danielson, L., & Rosenquist, C. (2014). Introduction to the TEC Special Issue on Data-Based Individualization. *TEACHING Exceptional Children, 46*(4), 6–12.

Fixsen, D. L., Blase, K., Horner, R., & Sugai, G. (2009). *Readiness for change* (Scaling-Up Brief No. 3). Chapel Hill, NC: Frank Porter Graham Child Development Institute.

Fixsen, D., Blase, K., Metz, A., & Van Dyke, M. (2013). Statewide implementation of evidence-based programs. *Exceptional Children, 79*(2), 213–230.

Fixsen, D. L., Blase, K. A., Timbers, G. D., & Wolf, M. M. (2001). In search of program implementation: 792 replications of the Teaching-Family Model. In G. A. Bernfeld, D. P. Farrington, & A. W. Laschied (Eds.), *Offender rehabilitation in practice: Implementing and evaluating effective programs* (pp. 149–166). London: Wiley.

Fixsen, D. L., Naoom, S. F., Blase, K. A., & Friedman, R. M. (2005). *Implementation research: A synthesis of the literature.* Tampa: University of South Florida, Louis de la Parte Florida Mental Health Institute.

Fuchs, D., Fuchs, L. S., & Stecker, P. M. (2010). The "blurring" of special education in a new continuum of general education placements and services. *Exceptional Children, 76*(3), 301–323.

Fuchs, D., Fuchs, L. S., & Vaughn, S. (2014). What is intensive instruction and why is it important? *Teaching Exceptional Children, 46*(4), 13–18.

Fuchs, L. S., & Fuchs, D. (1986). Effects of systematic formative evaluation: A meta-analysis. *Exceptional Children, 53*(3), 199–208.

Gandhi, A. G., Vaughn, S., Stelitano, L., Scala, J., & Danielson, L. (2015). Lessons learned from district implementation of intensive intervention: A focus on students with disabilities. *Journal of Special Education Leadership, 28*(1), 39–49.

Gischar, K. L., Hilt-Panahan, A., Clemens, N. H., & Shapiro, E. S. (2011). The process of implementation and design for sustainability. In E. S. Shapiro, N. Zigmond, T. Wallace, & D. Marston (Eds.), *Models for implementing response to intervention* (pp. 46–76). New York: Guilford Press.

Green, L. A., & Seifert, C. M. (2005). Translation of research into practice: Why we can't "just do it." *Journal of the American Board of Family Medicine, 18*(6), 541–545.

Individuals with Disabilities Education Act (IDEA), 20 U.S.C. §§ 1401 et seq. (2006).

National Center on Intensive Intervention. (2013). *Implementing intensive intervention: Lessons learned from the field.* Washington, DC: U.S. Department of Education, Office of Special Education Programs.

National Center on Intensive Intervention. (2015a). *DBI implementation rubric.* Washington, DC:

U.S. Department of Education, Office of Special Education Programs. Retrieved March 3, 2018, from *https://intensiveintervention.org/sites/default/files/dbi_implemenrubric_2015.pdf.*

National Center on Intensive Intervention. (2015b). *DBI implementation interview.* Washington, DC: U.S. Department of Education, Office of Special Education Programs. Retrieved March 3, 2018, from *https://intensiveintervention.org/sites/default/files/dbi_implemeninterview_2015. pdf.*

Pierce, J., & Ruedel, K. (submitted). *Hitting the ground running: What every teacher needs to know about results-driven accountability.*

Roehrig, A. D., Duggar, S. W., Moats, L., Glover, M., & Mincey, B. (2008). When teachers work to use progress monitoring data to inform literacy instruction: Identifying potential supports and challenges. *Remedial and Special Education, 29*(6), 364–382.

CHAPTER 6

Teaming Structures to Support Intensive Intervention Using Data-Based Individualization

Teri A. Marx
Steve Goodman

GUIDING QUESTIONS

> What existing teams can be leveraged for students receiving intensive intervention, and how do intensive intervention teams operate differently than existing teams?

> What strategies can be implemented to ensure efficiency and effectiveness of teams?

> What supports are needed for teams responsible for implementing intensive intervention?

Teaming—a term that refers to personnel coming together to collectively address similar goals—is based on the premise that individually, we may not know the answer but collectively, we have the solution. Working with professionals as a team can be an important part of a multi-tiered system of supports (MTSS) framework that includes response to intervention (RTI) and positive behavioral interventions and supports (PBIS), because teams function to ensure that students receive increasing levels of instructional and intervention support, based on need and guided by data. However, merely establishing a team does not ensure its functionality. Teams may have inefficiencies (e.g., 60 minutes for one student meeting) or a lack of understanding of how to effectively use data to identify specific supports for students, especially students with the most intensive needs.

At more intensive tiers of an MTSS framework, the data-based individualization (DBI) process can help teams implement efficient, data-driven student meetings (for more information about DBI within MTSS, see Bailey, Chan, & Lembke, Chapter 7, this volume). The DBI process, intended to support learners who are struggling the most, provides a structure for school teams to systematically review and analyze student-level data in order to strategically adapt, intensify, or individualize supports. DBI is not a "one-time" fix; rather, it is a process that relies heavily on a teaming structure and leverages expertise and perspectives from multiple school professionals and family members. We outline in this chapter (1) how teams utilizing the DBI approach operate differently from other school teams, (2) how team membership can positively impact DBI implementation, (3) responsibilities of team members to develop efficient structures, and (4) the types of supports needed for successful teaming.

TEAMING IN EDUCATION

Many educators are familiar with using teams to better support outcomes at the district, school, grade, or individual student levels. Educational teams encompass a group of individuals working together for a common purpose—to address a problem or improve educational outcomes. Teaming structures are common in schools implementing an MTSS framework, which aims to increase the likelihood that students will be successful in academics and/or behavior while reducing the probability of future problems. Within MTSS, teaming occurs for schoolwide improvement, student-level problem solving, and in special education. An example of various school teams, including their purposes, is provided in Appendix 6.1 and is available from the National Center on Intensive Intervention (NCII) and the National Center on Positive Behavioral Interventions and Supports (*https://intensiveintervention.org/resource/iep-teams*).

Schoolwide Improvement Teams

Within the school improvement process, teams focus on schoolwide efforts to improve the collective outcomes of academic and social-behavioral performance for all students, rather than on individual student problem solving. At this level (sometimes referred to as Core, Universal, or Tier 1), schools often put together a building leadership team that uses screening data to determine whether the majority of students (at least 80%) are responding to core instruction and are meeting schoolwide behavioral expectations. Leadership teams use data to determine how to improve instruction for all students—for example, they may review behavioral data indicating a pattern of more frequent student referrals during lunch. Based on this information, they may implement a precorrection strategy, reminding students of expected behaviors at lunch, as well as increase their reinforcement of expected behaviors during the lunch period (e.g., handing out more rewards/tokens). A more detailed discussion around the purpose and frequency of screening data is provided elsewhere (Burns, Riley-Tillman, & VanDerHeyden, 2012; Riley-Tillman, Burns, & Gibbons, 2013; McIntosh & Goodman, 2016). Pentimonti, Fuchs, and Gandhi (Chapter 2, this volume) provide further discussion of academic screening.

Problem-Solving Teams

As student data indicate a need to provide increased instruction/intervention, schools may develop a student support team whose purpose is to identify appropriate instructional strategies or interventions for individuals or groups of students. This team likely includes some overlap in membership from the schoolwide or building leadership team (e.g., administrator, teacher leaders, related service personnel). These student support or "problem-solving" teams (sometimes referred to as the Tier 2, MTSS, or intervention team) use progress monitoring data collected on small groups or individual students to determine student responsiveness to instruction and to identify next steps for supporting the student(s). Problem-solving teams operate differently across school settings but, typically, screening data are used to determine which students require additional instructional/intervention support across reading, math, and/or behavior. In some instances, a student referral to the student support team initiates the team's involvement. Problem-solving teams typically support the provision of *targeted* support and *intensive* support.

Targeted Support Teams

In a perfect world, student support teams at the targeted level of MTSS (i.e., Tier 2) would reflect on data for small groups of students receiving the same intervention to determine the groups' responsiveness. More often than not, however, teams review data on individual students to identify strategies for individualized needs. For many schools, individualizing supports at Tier 2 is not feasible given the sheer volume of students in need of/being referred for support.

Once students are identified for Tier 2 supports (i.e., targeted intervention or evidence-based strategy) and implementation begins, the problem-solving team may require that more frequent progress monitoring data (i.e., at least monthly), and other relevant data (e.g., work samples, entry/exit tickets, quiz/test scores) be collected. The team then sets a schedule to review how well students are responding to the Tier 2 supports in place, aligned with the duration of an intervention, and may adjust the intervention frequency, duration, or intensity if students are not responding to initial implementation.

Intensive Support Teams

At the stage at which more focused attention is given to an individual student (e.g., Tier 3 or special education), the problem-solving team may shift to a student-level team (i.e., student assistance, intensive support, individualized education program [IEP] team) that meets to identify appropriate supports for students with significant and persistent needs in academic and/or behavioral content domains. This is when the team may want to consider implementing the DBI process—especially if they have already made an initial change to the supports in place (i.e., adding intervention time, reducing group size). For many problem-solving teams, this is the point at which they experience difficulties in helping the student to make meaningful progress, and where DBI provides an opportunity.

Team membership will likely vary for each student receiving DBI/intensive supports, and membership may depend on available resources within the educational system or legal requirements. Because educators often participate in multiple teams and many times those teams serve a similar purpose, we suggest leveraging existing team members when meeting on students with intensive needs, rather than creating a separate team. This is particularly true when teams are already in place to improve outcomes for individual students with significant needs.

Legal Requirements and Considerations in Special Education

Schools are required by the Individuals with Disabilities Education Act (IDEA) to bring together multidisciplinary teams when evaluating students for suspected disabilities, and when developing and implementing an IEP for a student with an identified disability. The multidisciplinary team serves the function of determining eligibility for special education and developing an IEP that outlines the appropriate special education services and any ancillary services and transition plans.

The IEP, however, does not tend to specify the iterative cycles of instructional modifications that occur as a part of special education teaching practice. As such, DBI can help IEP teams develop more comprehensive support plans focused on addressing specific skill deficits in academics and social behavior. In addition to focusing on improving supports for individual students, intensive support teams and IEP teams share similarities in ensuring that there are individuals with expertise who represent multiple perspectives. While DBI may not be a mandated part of the IEP, its components are consistent with IEP requirements, and it can help teams be more efficient and data driven. And DBI has been shown to improve academic and/or behavior outcomes for students receiving special education services, making it especially valuable for students with disabilities, who historically have not made progress toward their IEP goals.

DBI THROUGH TEAMING

Although there may be perceived differences about the primary focus of various educational teams, the DBI process can improve the effectiveness of any intensive support team, including IEP teams, aimed at improving individual student outcomes. These teams aim to address individual student needs, which is a key feature of DBI. As teams implement the DBI process, they (1) analyze student assessment data, (2) develop a hypothesis for how to improve academic and/or behavior outcomes, (3) link assessment results to an individualized support plan, (4) monitor the effectiveness of the plan, and (5) continuously review data to ensure that outcomes are achieved (this may require revisiting earlier steps).

At the onset of the DBI process for an individual student, the team may require the collection of progress monitoring data even more frequently (e.g., biweekly, weekly, or daily [as appropriate]) than at the targeted level. The rationale for this increased frequency is to allow the team to intervene quickly when a student is not making adequate progress. Skilled intensive support teams utilizing DBI come to the table with graphs detailing student performance toward an individualized goal, as well as initial analyses of progress monitoring or other diagnostic data. The level of "prework" that occurs in the process can help intensive support teams shift conversations during meetings from "Let's look at the data" to "Let's use the data." This shift also moves the conversation from problem admiration to true problem solving—but it requires that the right people at the table are asking the right questions and using the right data to identify strategies. DBI, as an ongoing process, helps educators recognize that as school teams supporting struggling learners, it is our approaches that must change, not the student. And a team approach is critical to ensuring positive outcomes for students presenting with intensive and persistent needs.

DEVELOPING EFFICIENT AND EFFECTIVE TEAMING STRUCTURES

Intensive support teams plan how to customize individualized supports for students, especially students with chronically poor academic or behavioral performance, those being referred for special education, or those with identified disabilities. To build teaming efficiency, the intensive support teams should leverage the "heavy lift" of data collection/analysis and intervention tracking conducted by teams at earlier tiers, so that they can focus on how to adapt/intensify interventions or put supports in place. All the data collected, the records of attempted interventions, and conversations with parents/families and other practitioners gathered by a targeted support team can help expedite the DBI process for individual students.

Effective teams also define their goal or purpose; develop an action plan; and evaluate progress frequently, modifying their approaches as necessary. A summary of effective teaming components is presented in Table 6.1.

It is hard work to effectively address persistent challenges exhibited by students with significant needs. And while an individual teacher may apply the strategies of DBI for his or her student, the use of a team increases the probability of successful outcomes, especially when certain teaming conditions are in place. Teaming also provides encouragement and support for educators who implement intensive intervention through DBI given how involved the process may be. There are certainly benefits to the use of teams rather than addressing issues individually. Teams provide for greater variety of expertise and experience, which helps increase buy-in, reduce individual workloads by spreading tasks across multiple members, and ensure that progress is made in the right direction.

Team Membership for DBI

Given that intensive support teams are convened to support individual students with severe and/or persistent academic and/or behavioral needs, the team must include a variety of skilled practitioners, as well as personnel with the most in-depth knowledge

TABLE 6.1. Effective Teaming for Students with Intensive Needs

Ineffective teaming	More effective teaming	Most effective teaming (the DBI way)
Purpose		
Unclear understanding of the meeting purpose and desired outcomes	The meeting purpose and desired outcomes are discussed at the start of the meeting	All team members have a clear understanding of the meeting purpose and desired outcomes prior to attending the meeting
Structure		
No clear process for conducting the meeting or roles for participants	Use of a meeting agenda, with roles assigned at the meeting	Meeting agenda, graphed data, and team member role assignments are all established prior to the meeting
Problem-solving process		
Discuss problems/areas of needs	Discuss problems/areas of need and generate solutions	Following DBI process: review problems/ areas of need; generate hypotheses; match solutions to problem/area of need using progress monitoring, diagnostic, and fidelity data
Evaluation		
No evaluation on team effectiveness	Evaluation of tasks completed	Evaluation of student outcomes as related to DBI implementation, as well as annual evaluation of team effectiveness

of the child being supported through the DBI process. Bringing together professionals with different areas of expertise—and likely different perspectives—can prove invaluable when teams begin to identify how to intensify and individualize the supports for students going through the DBI process. The team should consist of members with advanced skills encompassing knowledge of the content area, knowledge of research and implementing evidence-based interventions, knowledge of valid and reliable progress monitoring tools, knowledge of how to use data to drive instructional adaptations, and knowledge of how to monitor fidelity to ensure successful implementation. Depending on school context, these roles may be filled by the same person or by different people.

Content Experts/Specialists

Content experts are the team members who understand deeply the content they are teaching and the pedagogy required for instructing hard-to-teach students. For example, a math content expert understands that algebraic reasoning begins with students having a strong number sense and may provide additional opportunities for a struggling learner to practice foundational skills in number sense through an explicit instructional sequence. This depth of knowledge is critical, as students with intensive needs—especially those who are working below grade level—often require intervention in foundational skills and in grade-level content.

Furthermore, many students who are "likely candidates" for the DBI process have both academic and behavioral skill deficits that need to be addressed (see Kuchle & Riley-Tillman, Chapter 3, this volume). Because of the interaction between behavior and academics, it is important to have team members with expertise across academic and behavioral domains. For example, a behavior specialist may be able to discern that a student's academic deficit is actually causing his or her escape/avoidance behavior (e.g., putting head on desk, asking to go to the bathroom), which is something on which an individual without behavioral expertise may not key.

Because content experts have integral understanding of the scope and sequence of either academic or behavioral skills, they may be the team member who can help identify the validated intervention program, evidence-based practice, or intensification strategy that will be most effective at addressing a targeted deficit area. And content experts ensure that an individual student's support plan has sufficient technical adequacy, by matching the best of scientific research to an individual student's need.

Importantly, the process of DBI itself may also be considered a content area. As such, intensive support teams should have professionals skilled in the DBI process. Team members with DBI content expertise may help facilitate meetings to ensure that the DBI process is followed. Additionally, DBI content experts may dually serve as the team's coach—ensuring that valid and reliable progress monitoring data are collected, graphed, and interpreted, so that the most appropriate interventions and strategies are implemented. In some instances, district-level personnel may serve in this capacity.

Interventionist

An *interventionist* is responsible for implementing an evidence-based practice or intervention, which may include delivering instruction and monitoring fidelity (i.e., implementing as intended). Many validated intervention programs specify the frequency and duration of the intervention, as well as information about *how* the intervention should be delivered. Interventionists should be trained in an intervention and knowledgeable about the implementation features specified by researchers or intervention developers to ensure they do not inadvertently render an intervention ineffective. It is also important to have the interventionist involved in developing a student's plan, as they can help determine things such as the setting for the intervention, the group size, the tools needed to monitor fidelity, and the timelines for data collection and review.

In many instances, the interventionist is the classroom teacher. However, other educators (i.e., special education teacher, reading specialist, related service provider, paraprofessional) may also serve as the interventionist. The educator delivering the intervention needs to have knowledge of the skill deficit area and how to deliver the intervention to address student deficits. Whoever serves in the role of the interventionist should understand the student's strengths and weaknesses, as well as his or her likes and dislikes. This knowledge is critical to ensuring the success of the intervention—if, for example, a student engages in attention-seeking behavior, an interventionist may want to select an intervention that allows the student frequent opportunities to respond, paired with immediate feedback, rather than selecting an intervention that is computer-based. The interventionist should also understand the environmental context in which the intervention is delivered, to better support a student with transferring a learned skill back to naturally occurring settings, such as a classroom.

Data Collectors and Interpreters

The first word in DBI is *data.* So intensive support teams must include members who are knowledgeable about valid and reliable progress monitoring tools, including how to administer and score measures. Individuals serving in this role are likely responsible for collecting and graphing data prior to team meetings. This allows time at the actual meeting to examine the student's level of responsiveness to determine whether adaptations to a student's support plan are needed. Often, general education teachers and interventionists administer and score progress monitoring measures and may graph data.

Because progress monitoring data are used to indicate *when* to make a change, not *how* to make a change (for additional discussion of assessment purposes, see Pentimonti et al., Chapter 2, this volume), intensive support teams should also include someone knowledgeable in interpreting progress monitoring data for responsiveness, as well as how to use the data diagnostically (i.e., conducting error analyses). Because DBI is centered around individual students, the team member responsible for data collection/ interpretation must also understand how to set individualized goals and graph data meaningfully—including the use of phase lines to indicate when changes are made to student plans. The person serving in this role may share the graphed data ahead of time to allow more time and energy to be directed toward addressing what the team can do if a student is not making adequate progress toward his or her goal. A school psychologist or special education teacher may have advanced training with data analysis and support the team with interpreting data.

When progress monitoring data cannot be used diagnostically without additional information—as may be the case with challenging behavior—the team may collect and bring additional diagnostic data, including data collected through a functional behavioral assessment. In these instances, a behavior specialist or related service provider (i.e., school psychologist or social worker) with expertise in behavioral principles may join the student's team.

Administrator (or Designee)

Administrators and other leaders in schools (e.g., instructional coaches, facilitators, veteran staff members) set the tone for successful DBI implementation. When leadership is supportive of not only the process but also those implementing the process, success is more likely. Administrators or administrative designees play an important role in ensuring that DBI is viewed as a priority. They also have decision-making authority and can ensure that resources—including personnel—are allocated sufficiently to support the various aspects of DBI implementation, including identification and purchase of evidence-based intervention materials; implementation supports (i.e., fidelity monitoring); and data collection and analysis tools, and resources. The administrator can also problem-solve and navigate issues stemming from state or district policy and guidance.

Family Members and Students

Two additional team members who are often either overlooked or underutilized within problem-solving processes are the students themselves and their family members. Since developing intensive support plans for students with significant need is complex and may have multiple iterations over the year, it is critical to gather information from those who know the student best. The family member is the adult that best knows the student and can contribute to suggestions about how to individualize an intervention. Family members, historically, are the strongest advocates for their child. They can share experiences across times, educators, and settings. They can provide a wealth of information to help identify features of a support plan that will increase the likelihood of success.

In many school settings, parent and family involvement may not be recognized as involvement by school personnel (Nelson & Guerra, 2009). However, parents and families can provide helpful information regarding history of mental health-related concerns, recent traumas or changes in the home environment, health issues, and/or educational services taking place outside of school hours, including tutoring or mentoring. Including parents and families in earlier tiers and helping them understand the DBI process may subsequently increase their involvement and engagement. Additionally, parents and family members may also act as liaisons to individuals who may be working with a student in settings outside of the school (e.g., church, community sports league, afterschool program). By involving parents and families, school personnel may be better positioned to reach out to others with influence in a child's life to gain additional insight/support for school plans.

While younger students may not be able to articulate why they are struggling with a specific skill, they may be able to provide information about which strategies may have more success. For example, a student may not want a specific type of strategy being used (e.g., verbal cues) for fear of stigma and may prefer an alternative approach (e.g., hand gesture or physical prompt). Without talking to that student, a team may never learn the student's preferences. Older students can offer similar information, and implementation may be more successful when they are involved in setting academic/behavioral performance goals and deciding on what types of strategies to include in their plan.

Other Team Members

As previously mentioned, DBI teams should be developed around the individual student for whom a plan is being developed. As a result, the DBI team for one student may look completely different than the team gathered for another student. In some instances, related service providers (e.g., speech pathologists, social workers, nurses) and/or interventionists/specialists (e.g., math, reading, or English language specialists; behavior interventionist) may be added to a student's team—either to support with collecting and/or analyzing data from a different perspective or to support with implementing interventions/adaptations. This may further differentiate how DBI teams operate differently from teams at earlier tiers, which often comprise a broader membership.

And if DBI is being used as a part of the IEP process for a student with a disability (or for a student going through the eligibility process), team membership may need to include other individuals required by IDEA. This may include special education teachers or providers; regular education teachers; a local educational agency representative; a transition agency representative; an individual who can interpret evaluation results (e.g., school psychologists); others with knowledge or expertise about the child, parents, or guardians; and the student as appropriate (Office of Special Education and Rehabilitative Services, 2000). Regardless of team membership, the goal is the same for every student involved in the DBI process—progress toward individualized goals.

RUNNING EFFECTIVE DBI MEETINGS

Throughout the DBI process, the goal is to ensure both efficiency and effectiveness. Utilizing standard agendas, establishing team member responsibilities, and outlining the problem-solving steps can increase the productivity of the intensive support team (see Figure 6.1).

Effective DBI meetings have a clear process and purpose to support students—and staff—to achieve desired outcomes. This involves starting meetings on time and following an agenda that focuses on individual student data and solutions. Using assessment data, the team considers what skills the student needs to work on and the best way to develop these skills through curriculum, instruction, and arranging environmental conditions to encourage successful responding. Since the team reviews data, it is helpful to summarize data in advance to make the best use of team members' time in problem solving. It is also helpful to have clear norms for how the meetings operate, as well as how decisions will be made. There are structured formats that teams in a problem-solving process can use (McIntosh & Goodman, 2016). These may include such

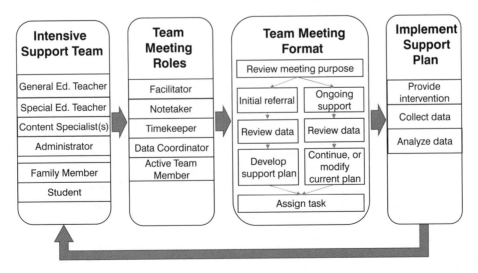

FIGURE 6.1. Schematic drawing of the intensive support team process to support implementation of DBI.

formalized meeting procedures as the team initiative problem-solving process (Newton, Todd, Algozzine, Algozzine, Horner, & Cusumano, 2014) or a 25-minute problem-solving process (Sprick, 1999).

Team Meeting Responsibilities

In addition to the roles previously discussed (e.g., content expert, interventionist, data collector, administrator), DBI teams often specify team member responsibilities to ensure meeting productivity. Assigning meeting responsibilities can help move meetings forward, ensuring adequate time for identifying next steps for both the student and for the staff members who work directly with the student. Some teams keep the assigned responsibilities consistent from one meeting to the next; other teams may rotate these functions among team members for each meeting.

Each meeting should have a *facilitator*. This individual creates the agenda, explains the purpose of the meeting, and keeps the participants on task. The facilitator may follow up with team members before or after meetings, identifying whether further information or support is needed. The facilitator may be a coach or administrative designee. His or her responsibility is to ensure that others understand what they need to do in *advance of the meeting* (e.g., administer and score progress monitoring measures, graph data, communicate with parents), *at the meeting* (e.g., clearly define student strengths and concerns, hypothesize strategies), and *after the meeting* (i.e., next steps).

Meetings should also have a *scribe or notetaker* who is responsible for taking informal notes and tracking brainstorming ideas in a visible space. This individual also documents formal notes using a template. During the meeting, the *data coordinator* is responsible for interpreting the data, and may suggest additional data be gathered to confirm initial analyses. Since it is easy to get "stuck" on certain items of the agenda, it is important to identify a *timekeeper*, whose function is to keep track of the times allocated for each section of the meeting and help the team members adhere to the allotted time. Any other personnel at the table serve as *active members*, listening and suggesting hypotheses or strategies to attempt.

Meeting Set-Up

Sufficiently preparing for a meeting is crucial to both productivity and efficiency. It seems obvious, but team members need to know when the meeting will take place; where it will be held; and the purpose of the meeting, including any tasks that should be completed in preparation. Unfortunately, participants may come to the meeting confused about these items. Teams should embrace an action-oriented, problem-solving approach that utilizes data for decision making. To efficiently act on information for decision making, data should be collected, analyzed, and summarized by a team member prior to the meeting.

In addition to having information and materials prepared for the meeting, teams may find it useful to have a computer and projector during the meeting when possible. This allows team members to view the same information being shared (e.g., student data, implementation data), as well as the notes being taken.

Standardized Agenda

The agenda and purpose of the meeting vary slightly depending on whether it is an initial meeting to develop supports for a student or a follow-up meeting to review student progress. When a standard agenda is in place (see Appendix 6.2), less energy is spent determining the meeting format, allowing more energy to be directed to problem solving and action planning. Additionally, consistent meeting structures help members predict the process and better prepare for participation. Some examples of standardized agenda items include (1) meeting purpose; (2) problem description; (3) sharing of data; (4) hypothesis development for a problem statement; and (5) action planning, including staff task assignments. It is important to identify time estimates for each part of the agenda so that the meeting can progress toward actionable next steps. Focusing too much time on problem description could lead to incorrect hypotheses, rushed decisions, or unassigned next steps. At first, time estimates may be quite "off base," but with practice, teams get more efficient and make more accurate estimates.

Meeting Schedules

With DBI, there are many factors to consider when setting meeting schedules. For efficiency, it is helpful to leverage existing meeting schedules whenever possible. Some schools may devote either a half-day or a full day—on a continuous cycle (every 6 weeks or quarterly)—for various teams to meet, rather than scheduling meetings across multiple days. They may structure the day parallel to the levels of support, beginning with meetings focused on schoolwide efforts, then move to targeted support team meetings, wrapping up with DBI/intensive support team meetings. This overlapping schedule may be beneficial when personnel are limited or when subcoverage is a concern. Developing a consistent teaming schedule, regardless of how it is operationalized in any given school, is critical.

At the intensive support level, teams may allocate different amounts of time for initial DBI meetings than for follow-up/monitoring meetings. The NCII (see Appendix 6.2) provides draft agendas for both types of meetings and includes suggested time allocations for each. For initial meetings on students with intensive needs, 30 minutes is suggested, with the bulk of the time spent identifying and prioritizing strategies to intensify existing interventions and establish next steps. At the initial meeting, team members may brainstorm multiple intensification strategies to try. The suggestions can help expedite future meetings, as teams will have a "bank" of strategies to consider if an initial approach is not successful. Follow-up/monitoring meetings, in that sense, should not take as long as initial meetings.

Because DBI is dependent on the implementation of an individualized plan and collecting/analyzing data to evaluate the success of the plan, meeting schedules should consider adequate time for the plan to be implemented. But, if meetings are held too frequently, the team may not be able to effectively evaluate whether a student is responding. Conversely, if meetings are held too far apart, teams may miss opportunities to intervene sooner. Also, teams should consider more frequent monitoring of student plans when problems are of higher concern or the student is at risk for continued failure.

Perhaps even more crucial than following agendas and schedules is monitoring what happens after the meetings. Assigned tasks must be completed. The intensive intervention strategies must be put into place. Data must be collected on student performance. And implementation fidelity for the intensive intervention must be monitored.

SUPPORTING TEAMS' USE OF DBI: THE ROLE OF THE DISTRICT

Schools can only go so far in supporting the effective implementation of DBI. Correct and effective DBI implementation requires resource allocation and the availability of staff with expertise in content and the DBI process. Supportive district policies ensure that intensive support teams use the DBI approach. Additionally, there is a need to continuously improve the skill sets of individuals who support students with the most intensive and persistent needs.

Commitment and Priority

District administration can support school-level intensive support teams through visibility and priority. Statements of commitment for the DBI approach helps to communicate the importance of this work and increase buy-in. District policy and resource allocation to support DBI demonstrates a commitment to serving students with challenging needs. The district can also ensure that effective policy is aligned with intensive intervention practice. This alignment is key when the classroom teachers and support staff members are negotiating multiple initiatives, including implementation of a new curriculum, using technology, or advocating for appropriate special education services.

Local Technical Expertise

District supports are critical for assisting educators who directly support students with intensive and persistent needs. Typically, teachers are generalist in their approach to providing instruction across content areas. As a result, the district may need to allocate staff members with specific content expertise (i.e., behavior specialists) for school-level team membership. The district can provide specialists in content areas, emphasizing the core features of intensifying supports that includes providing greater precision, engagement, practice, and feedback for the student receiving the supports.

Professional Development

The district may also provide professional development for educators through training and coaching. Training in key content—including the DBI process—is especially important if teachers did not receive adequate skill development during their teacher preparation coursework. It is also essential that veteran teachers and paraeducators receive training. Districts can also support ongoing professional development focused on the various aspects of DBI that educators may struggle with (e.g., data interpretation to individualize supports). To ensure that training effects are transferred to the classroom or student level, coaching may be an effective district support. Coaching can be viewed as a function rather than a position. Coaching focuses on prompting, fluency building, performance feedback, and adaptation of the new skill to the educational environment context (Massar, 2017). The teacher must also understand the core features of the intervention plan and be supported in implementation efforts so that the intervention is implemented with fidelity. A student may have an exemplary plan based on the best of science, but if the plan is not feasible or well implemented, we cannot expect optimal benefits for the student.

SUMMARY

We have discussed in this chapter the features of teams that develop and support an intensive individualized support plan through DBI, as well as how those teams can be structured to support successful DBI implementation. Using a team approach to implement the DBI process may be a new skill set; thus, it may take a while before team members develop proficiency with the process. Also, because it is a new skill set, it is important for the teams to be supported throughout this work. Implementing the DBI approach is intensive and takes resources, and should be reserved for supporting individual students with significant and persistent needs to ensure meaningful outcomes.

APPLICATION EXERCISE 6.1

Purpose

The following activity is intended to support district- and school-level personnel with reviewing available guidance and observing teaming practices to determine where and how to adopt the DBI process.

Review Existing Guidance

Review your school or district's existing guidance related to teams and reflect on how the guidance might be strengthened or modified. Consider these domains to develop guidance, if nothing is available.

Guiding Questions	In Place?	Reflection
Does your district/school have guidance outlined for *targeted support* teams?	☐	How comprehensive is the guidance?
Does your district/school have guidance outlined for *intensive support* teams?	☐	How comprehensive is the guidance?

Guiding Questions	In Place?	Reflection
Does your district/school have guidance outlined for *IEP* teams?	☐	How comprehensive is the guidance? How aligned is the guidance for *intensive support* and *IEP* teams?
Does your district/school have guidance about *who* should receive targeted, intensive, or special education supports?	☐	How comprehensive is the guidance? Are there identified decision rules (i.e., specific scores or performance metrics) for a student's movement between levels of supports?

Observe an Intensive Support/IEP Team Meeting

Observe an intensive support/IEP team meeting for an individual student to determine the extent to which there is a standardized process in place. Make recommendations for the team that may support more efficient team meetings.

    ☐ Intensive Support Team

    ☐ IEP Team

Meeting Start Time: _____

Meeting End Time: _____

Teaming Feature (check if in place)	Recommendations
Facilitator ☐ Scribe/notetaker ☐ Timekeeper ☐ Data coordinator ☐	
Agenda used during meeting ☐	
Times specified for agenda items ☐	
More time focused on identifying/ prioritizing strategies than on challenges ☐	
Data are graphed ☐	
Team hypothesized intensification strategies ☐	
Team identified and documented actionable next steps ☐	

Considerations for Adopting the DBI Process

Review the guiding questions to identify where and how the DBI process might be integrated into existing teaming structures/processes.

Guiding Questions	Response
Readiness and Buy-In	
What team, already in place in your school or district, can use the DBI approach? (Consider student support team, special education team, etc.)	
How can we develop interest within the team to apply the DBI process?	
What can be done to communicate with administration to support DBI implementation?	
How can we get access to DBI training for team members?	
How do we develop awareness for school staff members on what DBI is and how it will be beneficial for students and educators?	
How do we access the necessary resources, materials, and tools to implement DBI?	
Intensive Support Team Membership	
Who is our available content expert in academics and/or behavior?	
Who is our available data collector and data interpreter?	
Who is an interventionist that will be working with the student?	
Who will be the administrator (or administrative designee) assigned to the team?	
How will we involve parents/family members on the team?	
How will we involve the student on the team (when appropriate)?	

Guiding Questions	Response
Standardized Meeting Format	
Who will serve as the meeting facilitator (provides adequate information and materials before the meetings take place, including meeting information, agenda, computer projector)?	
How will we ensure that we follow the DBI process within our meeting agenda?	
Who will follow up to make sure that activities are monitored and accomplished?	

FREQUENTLY ASKED QUESTIONS

Is it possible to implement DBI without a team?

An educator (e.g., interventionist, general educator, or special educator) may implement the DBI process with individual students, especially if he or she is versed in data interpretation and identifying and implementing evidence-based practices and strategies. However, the quality of the DBI plan and implementation supports are likely increased through a team approach that includes members with various expertise and perspectives.

Can an IEP team use DBI?

Yes! While DBI may not be a mandated part of the IEP, its components are consistent with IEP requirements, and it can help teams be more efficient and data driven. IEP teams can use the DBI process to strengthen special education services by

- Encouraging more frequent review of progress monitoring data than minimally required for IEPs.
- Supporting multiple iterations of data-informed and evidence-based instructional adaptations as needed during the school year.
- Clearly articulating the intensity and individualization of specially designed instruction.
- Serving as the documented evidence for the "front-facing" IEP.

Where can we get training in DBI?

Individuals can learn more about DBI from the NCII website (*www.intensiveintervention. org*). Resources, implementation tools, and self-paced training modules are available on the NCII website. Additionally, the NCII works with several state educational agencies (i.e., departments of education) to develop their capacity to support the implementation of DBI. Check with your state to see if additional information is available.

REFERENCES

Burns, M. K., Riley-Tillman, T. C., & VanDerHeyden, A. M. (2012). *RTI applications: Vol. 1. Academic and behavioral interventions.* New York: Guilford Press.

Massar, M. M. (2017). *Effects of coach-delivered prompting and performance feedback on teacher use of evidence-based classroom management practices and student behavior outcomes.* Unpublished doctoral dissertation, University of Oregon, Eugene, OR.

McIntosh, K., & Goodman, S. (2016). *Integrated multi-tiered systems of support: Blending RTI and PBIS.* New York: Guilford Press.

Nelson, S. W., & Guerra, P. L. (2009). For diverse families, parent involvement takes on a new meaning. *National Staff Development Council, 30*(4), 65–66.

Newton, J. S., Todd, A. W., Algozzine, B., Algozzine, K., Horner, R. H., & Cusumano, D. L. (2014). Supporting team problem solving in inclusive schools. In J. McLeskey, N. L. Waldron, F. Spooner, & B. Algozzine (Eds.), *Handbook of research and practice for inclusive schools* (pp. 275–291). New York: Routledge.

Office of Special Education and Rehabilitative Services. (2000). A guide to the individualized education program. Retrieved from *www.ed.gov/offices/osers.*

Riley-Tillman, T. C., Burns, M. K., & Gibbons, K. (2013). *RTI applications: Vol. 2. Assessment, analysis, and decision making.* New York: Guilford Press.

Sprick, R. (1999). *25-minutes to better behavior: A teacher-to-teacher problem solving process.* Longmont, CO: Sopris West.

APPENDIX 6.1. How Can We Ensure That IEP Teams Provide the Most Intensive Supports?

DBI Process

Set individualized goals aligned to instructional outcomes

Pinpoint areas to target through specially designed instruction

Intensify academic and behavioral instruction based on data

Document instructional changes and fidelity

Use Data-Based Individualization (DBI) to Ensure IEP Implementation

Leverage a teaming structure*

Review IEP annually but progress monitor frequently

Communicate with and involve the family

Celebrate successes

Validated Intervention Program (e.g., Tier 2, Standard Protocol, Secondary Intervention)

Progress Monitor

RESPONSIVE

NONRESPONSIVE

Diagnostic Data

Intervention Adaptation

Progress Monitor

RESPONSIVE

NONRESPONSIVE

(continued)

Reprinted with permission from the National Center for Intensive Intervention at the American Institutes for Research. This resource was produced under the U.S. Department of Education, Office of Special Education Programs, Award Nos. H326Q160001 and H326S130004. Celia Rosenquist and Renee Bradley served as the project officers. The views expressed herein do not necessarily represent the positions or policies of the U.S. Department of Education. From Goodman, S., & Marx, T. A. (2018, July). How can we ensure IEP teams provide the most intensive supports? Retrieved from *https://intensiveintervention.org/resource/iep-teams*.

Teaming Structures across the Tiers

	Schoolwide (Core/Tier 1)	Targeted (Tier 2)	Intensive (Tier 3)	Individualized Education Program (IEP) Team
Key Questions	Is the core programming meeting the academic or behavioral needs of most students (e.g., 80% of students)?	Are the targeted supports meeting the academic or behavioral needs of students receiving targeted interventions?	Are the intensive supports meeting the academic or behavioral needs of students with intensive needs?	Are the special education supports and services appropriate and meeting academic or behavioral needs of students with IEPs?
Relevance to Data-Based Individualization	X	X	✓	✓
Team Membership	School/building leadership team, with subcommittees focused on academics and behavior (as needed)	Grade-level or problem-solving teams with representatives from school leadership team subcommittees (as needed)	Student-level team with representatives from problem-solving teams, and personnel with content and data analysis expertise	Similar to intensive support team, with additional members required by IDEA for a multidisciplinary team
Roles and Responsibilities	Develop plan, support implementation, and monitor the effectiveness of Core/Tier 1 programming	Develop plan, support implementation, and monitor the effectiveness of Targeted/Tier 2 programming	Develop plan, support implementation, and monitor the effectiveness of Intensive/Tier 3 programming	Determine special education eligibility, develop an IEP aligned with an intensive support plan, monitor the effectiveness of Intensive programming, and evaluate progress toward IEP goals
Data Sources	Benchmark/universal screening assessments, district assessments, state assessments, discipline referrals	Benchmark/universal screening assessments, progress monitoring measures, behavior "point sheets," discipline referrals	Academic diagnostic assessments, functional behavior assessment, individual student data across academics and behavior (e.g., work samples, anecdotal or observational data)	Use data from Tiers 1–3 with requirements for special education eligibility and programming (e.g., psychoeducational assessments, speech/language assessments, medical assessments and diagnoses)
Frequency of Data Collection/Data Review	Academics and behavior: Three times per year	Academics: One or more times per month Behavior: One or more times per week	Academics: One or more times per week Behavior: One or more times per day	Progress may use data collected in various tiers of support or may be specific to IEP goals; IEP must be reviewed at least annually

Initial Meeting Agenda
(30 minutes)

Note: *This is a sample protocol. Teams should modify the agenda as needed to fit their schedule, team structure, and so on.*

Roles	Recommended Team Members
• **Facilitator:** Explains the purpose of the meeting and keeps the participants on task. • **Referring Teacher:** Completes premeeting process, describes the student, and shares student data during the meeting. • **Scribe:** Takes informal notes and tracks brainstorming ideas in a visible space. • **Timekeeper:** Times each section of the meeting and helps the team adhere to the allotted time. • **Note Taker:** Takes formal notes for documentation using a template.	• Referring teacher • Intervention provider • Content specialist • Administrator • Coach • School psychologist • Social worker • Special educator • General educator/classroom teacher • Parent (as available and appropriate)

Step	Who	Time
Complete the Premeeting Form and bring graphed progress monitoring data, sample progress monitoring probes, relevant work samples, and other available diagnostic data.	*Referring teacher*	*Before meeting*
1. **Introduction and purpose**		2 min.
2. **Describe the student and share data**	Referring teacher	5 min.
3. **Ask clarifying questions to create hypothesis**	Team	5 min.
4. **Review evidence-based strategies for intensification**	Team	8–10 min.
5. **Prioritize and plan**	Team	5–7 min.
6. **Wrap-up and next steps**	Facilitator	3 min.

(continued)

Progress Monitoring Meeting Agenda
(15–30 minutes)

Note: *This is a sample protocol. Teams should modify the agenda as needed to fit their schedule, team structure, and so on.*

Roles	Recommended Team Members
• **Facilitator:** Explains the purpose of the meeting and keeps the participants on task. • **Intervention Provider:** Discusses implementation and student progress in the intervention. • **Scribe:** Takes informal notes and tracks brainstorming ideas in a visible space. • **Timekeeper:** Times each section of the meeting and helps the team adhere to the allotted time. • **Notetaker:** Takes formal notes for documentation using a template.	• Referring staff member • Intervention provider • Content specialist • Coach • Administrator • Classroom teacher • School psychologist • Social worker • Special educator • Parent (as available and appropriate)

Step	Who	Time
Compile and bring graphed progress monitoring data, sample progress monitoring probes, relevant work samples, and diagnostic data (if needed).	*Intervention provider*	*Before meeting*
1. **Summarize the student plan and discuss implementation of the plan**	Facilitator	2 min.
2. **Review progress monitoring data and additional data**	Intervention provider	3–7 min.
3. **Group questioning and hypothesis**	Team	3–5 min.
4. **Problem-solve, prioritize, and plan**	Team	5–10 min.
5. **Wrap-up and next steps**	Facilitator	2 min.

CHAPTER 7

Aligning Intensive Intervention and Special Education with Multi-Tiered Systems of Support

Tessie Rose Bailey

Gail Chan

Erica S. Lembke

GUIDING QUESTIONS

> Why should schools integrate data-based individualization within schoolwide multi-tiered systems of support?

> How does data-based individualization align with the essential components of multi-tiered systems of support?

> How can schools use data-based individualization to improve special education processes and outcomes for students with disabilities?

Schools in every state are implementing some form of a tiered system of support, whether it is called *multi-tiered systems of support* (MTSS), *response to intervention* (RTI), or *positive behavioral interventions and support* (PBIS).[1] Many schools begin implementation of a tiered system of support by focusing on components compatible with existing infrastructure, such as the delivery of core instruction at *Tier 1* and interventions at *Tier 2*. Focusing on Tiers 1 and 2 makes sense given that most students, around 90–95%, should benefit from these levels of instructional intensity. Regardless of our best efforts, however, evidence suggests that approximately 3–5% of students in the general population, often those with disabilities, and up to 30% of students not responding to Tier 1, will need more intensive support (Fuchs, Compton, Fuchs, Bryant, & Davis, 2008). *Data-based individualization* (DBI) gives schools the mechanism to provide these intensive supports and helps align special education with MTSS to create a robust schoolwide prevention model.

---

[1]Given that most states use MTSS, we use MTSS in this chapter to refer to tiered support models in academics and behavior.

Although MTSS implementation is widespread, implementation of DBI is not (Ruffini, Lindsay, McInerney, Waite, & Miskell, 2016). As you learned from Peterson, Danielson, and Fuchs (Chapter 1, this volume), DBI provides educators with a systematic, iterative decision-making *process* (i.e., not a single intervention) to intensify, adapt, and individualize instruction for students who do not make progress in Tier 2 interventions or on individualized education program (IEP) goals. Because DBI builds on existing components of an MTSS model—such as *progress monitoring*, Tier 2 interventions delivered with fidelity, and *data-based decision making*—it is more likely to be implemented successfully in schools with a well-functioning MTSS model in place (Gandhi, Vaughn, Stelitano, Scala, & Danielson, 2015). Thus, in this chapter we (1) demonstrate how DBI aligns with the essential components of MTSS, (2) provide considerations for implementing DBI within MTSS, and (3) model how DBI supports implementation of special education within an MTSS model.

ALIGNMENT OF DBI WITH ESSENTIAL COMPONENTS OF MTSS

Implementation of intensive intervention, and particularly DBI, depends on the same essential components necessary for successful MTSS implementation: a *multilevel prevention system, screening, progress monitoring,* and *data-based decision making* (see Figure 7.1). Given its dependence on these components, intensive intervention at *Tier 3* is often the last aspect of an MTSS model that schools implement. Not surprisingly, it is also considered the most difficult, especially when schools do not have the necessary MTSS

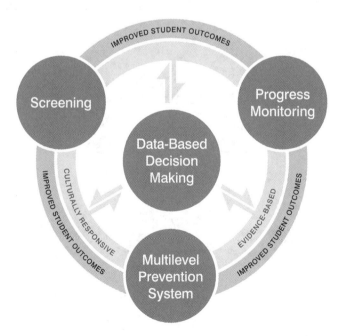

FIGURE 7.1. MTSS framework and essential components. Reprinted with permission from the Center on Response to Intervention at the American Institutes for Research (2010).

infrastructure in place (Ruffini et al., 2016). Implementing DBI within an existing MTSS model can help schools avoid common implementation challenges and facilitate timelier implementation. In this section, we demonstrate how each of the components supports and improves DBI implementation.

MTSS Essential Components

Multilevel Prevention System

An MTSS model includes varying levels of support, though the most common approach uses three increasingly intense levels of intervention and support, referred to as the multilevel prevention or instructional system. This multilevel system is commonly presented as a triangle (see Figure 7.2) with three tiers. DBI is associated with the most intensive tier, or Tier 3. As demonstrated in Figure 7.2, the success of services and supports delivered at Tier 3 rests on successful implementation of less intensive tiers. In effective MTSS models, different tiers of support are clearly defined by the level of support provided to the student, as opposed to the intervention. Failure to distinguish tiers from each other can result in students not receiving necessary supports in a timely manner. Table 7.1 provides descriptions of the distinguishing characteristics of supports in each tier. We present below a brief description of how DBI connects to each tier.

TIER 1: THE INSTRUCTIONAL FOUNDATION OF MTSS

Tier 1, or core instructional programming, serves as the foundation of the instructional prevention model and is expected to meet the needs of most students (~80%). At Tier 1, teachers utilize research-based practices that are likely to have a high impact on student

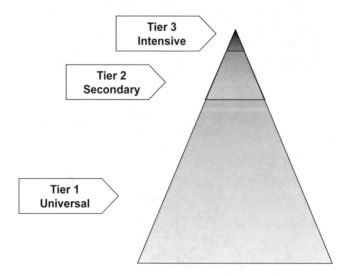

FIGURE 7.2. Visual representation of the MTSS instructional tiers. Reprinted with permission from the National Center on Intensive Intervention at the American Institutes for Research (2018).

TABLE 7.1. Comparison of MTSS Levels of Instructional Support

	Tier 1	Tier 2	Tier 3
Instruction/intervention approach	Comprehensive research-based curriculum	Standardized, targeted small-group instruction	Individualized and adapted interventions based on student data, or DBI
Group size	Classwide (with some small-group instruction)	Three to seven students	No more than three students (ideally)
Monitor progress	Once per term	At least once per month	Weekly
Population served	All students	At-risk students	Students with significant and persistent needs

Note. Reprinted with permission from the National Center on Intensive Intervention at the American Institutes for Research (2013b).

learning. In earlier chapters, you learned that DBI focuses on providing interventions designed to address basic skills deficits preventing the student from progressing in the general curriculum. All students, including those receiving DBI at Tier 3 or in special education, still require access to core content standards available through Tier 1 instruction. In some cases, this may require teachers to provide accommodations, alternative learning environments, modified curriculum, and assistive technology.

TIER 2: THE PLATFORM FOR DBI

DBI is dependent on a Tier 2 system that uses a validated intervention platform that can be intensified when students are not making sufficient progress (see Peterson et al., Chapter 1, this volume). Within MTSS, this validated intervention platform, sometimes referred to as an *evidence-based intervention,* is delivered to small groups of students using standardized interventions. When schools select Tier 2 interventions with standard protocols for delivery, they are more likely to maximize resources, increase immediate access to supports, increase fidelity of implementation, decrease training

---

Resources for Selecting Tier 2 Interventions to Support DBI

- **National Center on Intensive Intervention Tools Chart** (*www.intensiveintervention.org*)
  - ○ Academic Intervention Tools
  - ○ Behavior Intervention Tools
- **What Works Clearinghouse** (*https://ies.ed.gov/ncee/wwc*)

costs, and improve student outcomes (Fuchs, Mock, Morgan, & Young, 2003). Given the importance of Tier 2 interventions in successful DBI implementation, schools should select Tier 2 interventions with evidence demonstrating significant gains for most students. Using validated interventions at Tier 2 allow educators to intensify existing interventions in both academics and behavior as opposed to implementing a new intervention. In addition, implementing a validated Tier 2 intervention that will likely meet the needs of most at-risk students reduces the number of students in need of intensive intervention. There are many resources available to support school teams in identifying Tier 2 interventions that will also support DBI implementation at Tier 3.

TIER 3: DBI

Tier 3, the most intensive level of MTSS intervention, is considered the most challenging for schools in terms of achieving fidelity and appropriate intensity (Danielson & Rosenquist, 2014; Gandhi et al., 2015; Ruffini et al., 2016). DBI offers schools a systematic, empirically tested approach for designing and individualizing instruction and behavioral supports. It is an effective strategy for improving outcomes for students with severe learning needs (see Fuchs & Fuchs, 1998; Stecker, Fuchs, & Fuchs, 2005). Using a systematic process such as DBI for Tier 3 can help schools efficiently and effectively provide intensive intervention for students in general and special education settings. For more detail about how DBI looks when implemented as Tier 3, see Peterson et al. (Chapter 1, this volume).

Universal Screening

With screening, schools use brief, valid, and reliable tools to identify students who are at risk for poor learning and behavioral outcomes. While most screening tools are validated to identify students for Tier 2 levels of support, recent research has shown that universal screening may help identify which students need the most intensive intervention. Teams may use screening decision rules that fast-track students with the weakest initial skills by skipping Tier 2 instruction and moving directly into intensive

---

Resources for Selecting MTSS Progress Monitoring and Screening Tools That Support DBI

- **National Center on Intensive Intervention Tools Charts**
  (*www.intensiveintervention.org*)
  - Academic Screening Tools
  - Behavior Screening Tools
  - Academic Progress Monitoring Tools
  - Behavior Progress Monitoring Tools

  For more in-depth information about assessment, see Pentimonti, Fuchs, and Gandhi (Chapter 2, this volume).

intervention. There is growing evidence that this early identification and provision of intensive intervention results in significantly stronger academic performance for those who move linearly through the tiers (Al Otaiba, Wagner, & Miller, 2014; Fuchs, Fuchs, & Compton, 2012). To support DBI implementation, schools must select valid and reliable screening tools that allow for early identification of the most at-risk students. Most schools select a comprehensive MTSS assessment system with tools for conducting screening and progress monitoring. School teams should select MTSS assessment systems that can support assessment and decision making at all levels of instruction, including DBI at Tier 3. Rather than screening all students in a building at the secondary school level, universal screening might include a review of data that are already available (e.g., state test scores from the previous year) followed by administration of a validated screening tool for those deemed to be at risk. For further information about assessment, see Pentimonti et al. (Chapter 2, this volume).

Progress Monitoring

As part of a comprehensive MTSS assessment system, schools use progress monitoring to confirm risk status (Center on Response to Intervention, 2010), quantify rates of improvement and inform instructional practice (Center on Response to Intervention, 2012), and intensify academic and behavioral interventions through DBI (National Center on Intensive Intervention [NCII], 2013a). When DBI is aligned with MTSS, teams use the same types of progress monitoring tools at Tier 2, Tier 3, and special education. Using the same MTSS progress monitoring tools for DBI, Tier 2, and special education can improve student transitions among the tiers, create more efficient data decision-making processes, and maximize resources. It is recommended that teams use the tools charts published by the NCII to identify progress monitoring tools appropriate for use across academics and behavior at Tier 2 (e.g., monthly to biweekly administration) and Tier 3 (e.g., weekly to daily administration). For students at the secondary school level, progress monitoring is perhaps one of the most essential features of the MTSS system. Progress monitoring ensures that students' academic needs are being met through ongoing collection and use of data in a setting where students have more autonomy and less oversight than at lower grade levels. For more information about using progress monitoring in DBI, see Pentimonti et al. (Chapter 2, this volume).

Data-Based Decision Making

As shown in Figure 7.1, effective data-based decision making is central to implementation of the other three MTSS essential components: screening, progress monitoring, and multilevel prevention system. Similarly, data-based decision making is central to DBI implementation. Data-based decision making within MTSS requires that teams at all levels, including intensive support teams, have access to a data system that allows users to document, graph, and access student-, grade-, and school-level data. Like Tier 2 teams, intensive support teams, sometimes called *DBI teams*, need access to graphed progress monitoring data that include a goal line, a trendline, and phase lines. Research suggests that six to nine data points are sufficient to make academic instructional decisions. With behavior, the number of data points is not as well researched. As a general rule of thumb for behavior, a minimum of three data points and a review of level and trend are appropriate (Wehby, 2013). If variability is observed in behavior data while using DBI, consider collecting a few more data points. If after five data points, performance or progress is not changing as expected (i.e., a decrease in problem behavior or an increase in appropriate behavior), it is worth considering a reevaluation and adaptation of the current intervention.

Because the assessment tools are the same, MTSS teams at Tiers 2 and 3, as well as in special education, should also use consistent criteria for determining whether students are responding to an intervention and whether a change to the intervention is needed. At the middle school level, a common structure for decision making is the use of interdisciplinary, grade-level team meetings. Each team may include a content-area teacher from each subject area, a special education teacher, and perhaps a school counselor, school psychologist, or interventionist. These teams meet frequently to discuss student data and to determine whether intervention modifications are needed for individual students. At the high school level, teams might also include content-area specialists across grades, but the team discussions are similar to those in middle school. Marx and Goodman (Chapter 6, this volume) provide more information on the role of teams when implementing DBI.

IMPLEMENTING DBI WITHIN MTSS

In addition to aligning DBI with the essential components of MTSS, schools can improve the efficiency of implementation by aligning features of successful DBI and MTSS implementation. Such features include data teams, intervention scheduling, and documentation procedures.

Aligning MTSS and DBI Data Teams

Aligning MTSS and DBI teams is important for maximizing resources, time, and staff expertise. It is important to remember that other teams, including the school implementation team and Tier 2 teams, refer students who are not responding to intervention to the intensive support team, or DBI team. As a result, schools are encouraged to select team members who can serve on other teams as well. This overlapping of staff members supports a seamless transition of students among different levels of intensity of support and movement through the special education process, if needed. Given that staff members serve on multiple teams, it will be important to use consistent meeting processes, including consistent team norms, documentation procedures, and similar data storage formats (e.g., data dashboards, Google drives). These shared processes allow for greater collaboration across teams and efficiency in the teaming process. Intensive support team meetings should be included on the master schedule with other MTSS team meetings.

Although the intensive support team should align with other MTSS teams, its function should be distinguishable from these other teams. The intensive support team's primary responsibility is to monitor the DBI process for students who have not responded to interventions at Tier 2 or in special education. Unlike other MTSS teams, teachers or interventionists delivering the DBI intervention regularly attend meetings to present data about their students. If teachers bring data to meetings, intensive support teams may spend 20–30 minutes per student moving through the DBI process. As a result, intensive support teams are likely to meet more frequently than other MTSS teams (e.g., weekly and biweekly). For an in-depth discussion about teaming and DBI, see Marx and Goodman (Chapter 6, this volume) or check out the NCII website (*www.intensiveintervention.org*) for adaptable forms and processes to assist intensive support teams in implementing efficient data meetings.

Scheduling Intervention

Scheduling intervention for students with learning and/or behavior problems is a common challenge for DBI and MTSS implementation. Effective school MTSS schedules support multiple levels of intervention and high-quality instruction based on the needs of the student population. Implementing a system of increasingly intense interventions is easiest when schools designate a specified time during the school day for intervention. Adequate time, at least 30–45 minutes each day, ensures that interventions can be sufficiently intensified as needed. DBI and Tier 2 interventions can be delivered during the same intervention block, but this may create challenges in situations in which students are receiving a Tier 2 intervention in one subject and DBI in another. Schools may schedule multiple shorter intervention blocks, such as three 20-minute blocks, to allow for distributed practice across the school day or to allow students in need of DBI in one area to receive intervention in another area of need. The intervention schedule should be flexible to support changes to student groupings, intervention duration, and frequency of delivery, as needed. At the secondary school level, there are several ways to build intervention into a daily schedule. Often, schools have a homeroom time at the start of the day, in which individual needs, goal setting, and schoolwide expectations can be discussed. This can be an effective time to deliver intervention to small groups, if structured correctly. Intervention can also be built into supervised *learning labs* if more than one special education teacher is available. Finally, intervention can be built into the daily schedule as an elective option for all students who are at risk.

DBI Documentation

Within MTSS, teams must document efforts to intervene with students identified as being at risk. This documentation may be used to record prior efforts, to make *referrals* to special education, to plan interventions, to develop IEPs, to design specially designed instruction and services, and to engage in program evaluation. Cumbersome or redundant paperwork can create frustration among educators and can prevent them from providing important information. To the extent possible, teams should align DBI documentation efforts with existing procedures used at Tier 2 and in special education. DBI documentation should be housed with other data sources within a comprehensive MTSS data system. To support intervention and teaming at all levels of instruction, data systems should allow educators to view current and past intervention efforts used with students. In some cases, schools may not have identified effective or efficient documentation approaches. The NCII offers a set of tools to assist educators in documenting the intensive intervention plan, implementation fidelity, and intensification efforts. Appendix 7.1 includes a sample form from the NCII that educators can use to easily document daily implementation fidelity of DBI and record the results of problem solving at the end of each week.

One critical aspect of documentation is fidelity. Schools and districts have expressed difficulty with consistently monitoring fidelity of DBI assessments and academic and behavioral intervention procedures. In addition, schools and districts have struggled to apply data decision rules consistently for intensifying instruction through DBI within MTSS (Arden, Gandhi, Zumeta Edmonds, & Danielson, 2017). Documentation of fidelity should be collected during implementation of intervention at all levels of intensity, but it is essential for decision making at Tier 3. The following scenario helps explain why documentation of DBI fidelity is so important:

> Mrs. Adams is implementing an intensive intervention focused on increasing decoding skills to Johanna and two other students each day for 30 minutes. The intervention includes systematic phonics instruction for 10 minutes, reading out of decodable readers for 10 minutes, individual and choral sound checks for 5 minutes, and review of tough sounds for the last 5 minutes. Because the school has limited intervention space, Mrs. Adams delivers the intervention in an alcove close to the second-grade hallway. Each day, Mrs. Adams documents the attendance and engagement of the students using the DBI daily implementation log (see sample in Appendix 7.1) and indicates the degree to which the intervention was delivered as planned. She also collects weekly progress monitoring data to assess Johanna's progress toward her goal. Based on the progress monitoring data collected over the last couple of weeks, the team determines that Johanna is not progressing in the intensive intervention. Before considering a change to the intervention, the team reviews the daily implementation fidelity data collected by Mrs. Adams (see Figure 7.3). What do you notice about the implementation data?

Too often, educators fail to consider how well the intervention was delivered and the interplay of academic and behavioral issues before deciding to make an intervention change or refer a student for more intensive intervention or special education. At Tier 2, this can result in some students being inappropriately referred for intensive intervention. At Tier 3, this can lead to selecting a mismatched intervention and/or inappropriate referrals to special education. Both situations can be costly. By aligning procedures for documenting fidelity of progress monitoring and intervention implementation at all levels, educators can more accurately identify why students may not be responding to the intervention and thus develop more appropriate solutions. In the previous scenario, the availability of fidelity data assists the teachers in understanding why Johanna may not be responding. Without these data, the intensive support team would not have known that Johanna's behavior (i.e., attendance and inconsistent engagement) rather than the intervention components, may be contributing to her lack of progress. Access to the fidelity data allows the team to more efficiently identify how to support Mrs. Adams. For example, the team may help her develop a behavior plan for increasing

Daily Intervention Log

Please fill out this log each day. If an intervention is not scheduled for a given day or could not be offered (e.g., holiday, your absence), then please mark "N" under the column "Intervention Offered?" and leave the rest of the row blank. On days when the student receives intervention (Student Present? = Y), indicate the duration (minutes) or frequency (e.g., number of check-ins) of the intervention, rate the extent of student engagement, and rate the plan implementation.

Day	Intervention Offered	Student Present	Intervention Duration or Frequency	Was the Student Engaged No Partially Yes	Was the Intervention Implemented as Planned No Partially Yes
Monday	☑ Y ☐ N	☐ Y ☑ N	—	☐ 1 ☐ 2 ☐ 3	☐ 1 ☐ 2 ☐ 3
Tuesday	☑ Y ☐ N	☑ Y ☐ N	30 min	☐ 1 ☑ 2 ☐ 3	☐ 1 ☐ 2 ☑ 3
Wednesday	☑ Y ☐ N	☑ Y ☐ N	25 min	☑ 1 ☐ 2 ☐ 3	☐ 1 ☐ 2 ☑ 3
Thursday	☑ Y ☐ N	☑ Y ☐ N	30 min	☐ 1 ☐ 2 ☑ 3	☐ 1 ☑ 2 ☐ 3
Friday	☑ Y ☐ N	☐ Y ☑ N	—	☐ 1 ☐ 2 ☐ 3	☐ 1 ☐ 2 ☐ 3

FIGURE 7.3. Sample completed daily intervention log.

Johanna's attendance and engagement. Monitoring fidelity at Tier 1 and Tier 2 is equally important, and teams should ensure that data collection processes are aligned for more efficient and timely data collection.

IMPROVING SPECIAL EDUCATION THROUGH DBI AND MTSS

Tiered systems of support were originally intended to support appropriate identification of students with disabilities. However, experts have observed that schools implementing tiered systems often focus on core instruction and may treat special education as a separate system (Arden et al., 2017). This is unfortunate because early research suggested that tiered systems of support can lead to improvements in the special education system, including decreases in rates of disproportionality in special education, inappropriate special education referral and placement rates, and the length of needed special education services (Burns, Appleton, & Stehouwer, 2005; Dexter, Hughes, & Farmer, 2008; VanDerHeyden, Witt, & Gilbertson, 2007). Implementing DBI within MTSS can further assist schools in aligning special education requirements within the larger schoolwide prevention framework. In effective MTSS models, educators view special education as part of the prevention services available to eligible students across the tiers of instruction. When used as part of Tier 3, DBI can assist teams in meeting Individuals with Disabilities Education Act (IDEA) *Child Find* requirements and making eligibility determination decisions. For students receiving special education, DBI can support the provision of specially designed instruction across the continuum of services, since the components of the DBI process align with IEP requirements (e.g., specially designed instruction, progress monitoring, individualized goals).

Using DBI for Special Education Referral and Eligibility Determination

An advantage of integrating DBI into Tier 3 of an MTSS model is that it allows teams to streamline the Child Find procedures for identifying students with learning disabilities. Under the IDEA (34 CFR § 300.111), local education agencies, or districts, are responsible for identifying, locating, and evaluating students with disabilities who need special education. DBI provides teams with a systematic process for supporting students who fail to respond to intervention supports and may require ongoing data-driven, individualized instruction and supports to progress toward the standards. It may also assist in identifying students who might be making some progress, but the level of instructional intensity necessary to achieve that level of progress can only be delivered through special education. In other words, DBI data can provide evidence demonstrating that a student requires specially designed instruction to access and progress in the general education curriculum (i.e., standards), which is a critical component of special education eligibility determination.

Educators should check their state's special education regulations for specific rules impacting how the intensive support team implements Child Find procedures within MTSS. Neither MTSS (including RTI) nor DBI can be used to delay or deny a referral to special education, and parents may still request a comprehensive evaluation at any time (see Memorandum to State Directors, 2011).

With respect to special education eligibility, the most recent reauthorization of IDEA recognizes "a process that determines if the child responds to scientific, research-based intervention" as an approach for identifying students with specific learning disabilities (§ 1414[b][6][B]; §§ 300.307, 300.309, and 300.311). This process is commonly referred to as RTI in the literature and in some state policies and procedures. RTI for eligibility determination should be embedded within schoolwide MTSS implementation to ensure that students receive access to appropriate instruction in reading and math [34 CFR § 300.309(a)]. Furthermore, when DBI is situated within MTSS, it can provide essential data to support eligibility determination decisions. Documentation of a student's participation in DBI can assist teams in determining whether a student *needs* special education. The data-driven intensification process embedded within DBI mirrors specially designed instruction available through special education. A student who requires ongoing DBI, which cannot be feasibly delivered within the general education context, may be a student who needs special education. Progress monitoring data collected during DBI may also provide evidence of a student's lack of response to standardized and intensified interventions that can be shared with parents and families, a requirement for referral under the use of RTI for eligibility determination (34 CFR § 300.311).

Accurate goal setting is essential for using DBI as part of the special education referral and eligibility processes. Goals that are set too low may prevent some students from accessing needed special education services in a timely manner. Goals that are set too high given the student's baseline data may lead teams to refer students who are making significant progress but cannot meet the goal within the unrealistic time frame. Using grade-level rate of improvement (ROI) norms helps teams assess whether the student can progress at the same rate as his or her same-age peers. Referral and eligibility teams can use this information to document that the student is unable to meet grade-level expectations through general education supports alone, even when provided additional intensive intervention. See Pentimonti et al. (Chapter 2, this volume) for more information about progress monitoring and goal setting.

Data collected through DBI are one of many data sources teams may use to determine eligibility for special education. As required under IDEA, observations in the general education setting are conducted in the area(s) of suspected disability. In addition, the team must address exclusionary factors, such as ruling out persistent and negative behavior or intellectual disabilities (34 CFR § 300.311). With respect to eligibility determination using an RTI process, one approach involves identifying whether a student has a specific learning disability as evidenced by both a slow rate of progress and an overall low performance level at the end of two rounds of interventions (Hughes & Dexter, 2015). During the eligibility determination process, the student should continue to participate in DBI to prevent further loss of learning. If the student is found to be eligible for special education, he or she will continue to receive specially designed instruction through DBI, until he or she demonstrates adequate progress on his or her IEP goals.

The following scenario highlights how one district used DBI within an MTSS framework to support teams in making decisions about referral and eligibility for special education. Although the decision to provide intensive intervention using DBI, or to refer a student for a special education evaluation, may occur at any time, the following fictitious example uses the benchmarking time period to provide a relatively straightforward illustration of the process.

> Johnson School District's approach to using MTSS to support the special education referral process aligns with state regulations and guidelines. To increase consistency in implementation, the district refined decision-making criteria and assigned a school psychologist at each school to lead the process. The process begins with data. At each benchmark period, the grade-level problem-solving team examines screening and progress monitoring data to identify students who either are not making adequate progress in their current Tier 2 intervention or fall below the 10th percentile compared to grade-level national norms. The team uses additional data (e.g., other valid screening or progress data, state assessments, behavior, attendance, work samples, or other available standardized test data) to verify whether students are significantly at risk for poor learning outcomes. If data confirm that a student is significantly at risk, the team members prepare to provide intensive intervention using DBI. At this point, they may also decide to refer a student for a comprehensive evaluation to determine special education eligibility if they suspect a disability based on the data noted earlier, and their knowledge about the student.
>
> Once a student is identified for intensive intervention, the intensive support team develops an intervention plan matched to the student's needs, sets a progress monitoring goal, and identifies a time to review the data. Then, the interventionist (and other team members, as appropriate) delivers the intervention and documents adherence to fidelity using a log. The interventionist also collects progress monitoring data every week to determine whether the student is making sufficient academic progress in the intervention.
>
> If a student is not making adequate progress, the team reviews the intervention log to confirm that it was delivered as intended. Once the team members verify that the intervention was delivered appropriately, they move through the DBI

process to further intensify the student's intervention plan. To indicate a change in the intervention, the team members add a phase line to the progress monitoring graph, and set a date to meet to review progress data (e.g., after 6 weeks). When the team members reconvene, they review the data to determine whether the student's progress has improved with the increasingly individualized, intensive intervention. If the student is making sufficient progress, the team members continue to implement the successful intervention plan, and the interventionist continues to collect weekly progress monitoring data. If progress is insufficient, the team members return to the data to determine how to further intensify the intervention plan.

It is important to note at this point that the team has both progress data about the student and information about the level of support needed to facilitate progress (or the lack thereof). This information is critical, because it can inform decisions to either refer a student for a comprehensive evaluation or determine eligibility for special education and the need for specially designed instruction, if an evaluation is already under way.

DBI and Students Receiving Special Education Services

The intent of special education is to provide eligible students opportunities to make progress beyond the tiered supports provided only through general education. DBI, when used at Tier 3 and in special education, can support schools in enhancing the quality of special education services by providing teachers a data-driven process for designing and delivering specially designed instruction based on student need. Data collected throughout the DBI process, including progress monitoring and diagnostic data, can assist IEP teams in writing accurate, data-based present-level statements, as well as ambitious but realistic IEP goals. Ongoing use of progress monitoring through DBI assists special education teachers in evaluating and sharing students' progress toward IEP goals. DBI provides for special education teachers a process that allows them to use validated approaches to intensify specialized instruction for students who are not making adequate progress in academic and behavior areas. As previously mentioned, DBI supports the design and implementation of specially designed instruction available within a continuum of support. Special education teachers are encouraged to collaborate with other general and special education colleagues to problem-solve ways to intensify instruction and behavioral supports for students with disabilities who are not progressing on one or more IEP goals. Too often, special education teachers lack access to teacher problem-solving teams with whom they can share data for students with disabilities who are struggling. Aligning intensive intervention problem-solving teams can increase collaboration among special education and general education teachers to support all students with intensive needs.

SUMMARY

As our understanding of effective implementation has evolved, so has our belief that to support all students, schools must begin to align the various support systems within a schoolwide MTSS model. As you have learned throughout this chapter and others in this book, DBI has the potential to improve outcomes for students with the most significant learning and behavioral needs, including students with disabilities. To maximize the effects of DBI implementation, schools must be intentional and strategic in their approach to aligning DBI with the essential components of MTSS and special education (see Arden et al., 2017; NCII, 2013a). DBI enhances both special education and MTSS implementation by providing schools with a systematic process for providing intensive intervention and supports for general and special education students. It also provides schools with a validated approach for locating and identifying students who may need special education and assists special education teachers in designing and implementing specially designed instruction for eligible students. The power of using DBI to enhance MTSS and special education is that it helps provide a bridge between special education and general education services, often viewed as two separate systems, to support schools in implementing a comprehensive, schoolwide prevention model.

APPLICATION EXERCISE 7.1. Selecting Assessment Tools That Support DBI within MTSS

Effective implementation of DBI uses existing structures often available within MTSS, such as evidence-based interventions and assessment tools. For this activity, access the NCII academic screening and progressing monitoring tools charts (*www.intensiveintervention.org*). With a team, select two to three tools and compare the extent to which they support implementation of DBI within MTSS. Consider the following:

1. Is the tool part of a comprehensive MTSS data system that includes progress monitoring and screening tools?
2. Is there evidence that the screening tool allows students to fast-track to DBI and bypass Tier 2?
3. Does the progress monitoring tool support implementation of DBI?

Using the data collected by the team, select which tool appears to best support alignment of DBI within MTSS. Share your rationale with other groups.

APPLICATION EXERCISE 7.2. Should We Refer the Student for Special Education Testing?

Determining whether to refer a student for a special education comprehensive evaluation is not always an easy decision. Teams must review all the available data and determine whether a referral for special education testing is warranted. In teams of three to four, review the fictitious scenarios below and come to consensus about whether your team would consider making a special education referral.

Scenario 1. Sarah is a fourth grader who scored at the 27th percentile on the fall reading screening assessment. During the spring semester of third grade, she participated in a small-group intervention with six other students. Unlike most of the students in the intervention, she did not make adequate progress toward her goal. Because it was close to the end of the school year, the third-grade team members decided they would recommend that the fourth-grade team fast-track her to a more intensive intervention. As a result, Sarah began receiving a moderately intense intervention delivered by the reading specialist soon after the start of fourth grade. As part of the progress monitoring plan, the fourth-grade team members set the goal using a grade-level ROI of 0.8 words read correctly. After 6 weeks, the team members reconvened and reviewed Sarah's progress and found her ROI during the intervention was only 0.6 words read correctly. The team reviewed fidelity data and determined that the intervention was delivered as intended.

You and your two to three colleagues are the new fourth-grade team. With your team, discuss the following questions and come to a consensus about whether your team would recommend that Sarah be referred for special education, providing a rationale for your team's decision:

1. What information from the scenario might suggest a referral is appropriate?
2. What information from the scenario might suggest there are insufficient data to support a referral?
3. Should the team consider a referral for a special education evaluation? Why or why not?
4. What other next steps might the team recommend?

Scenario 2. Bobby is a second-grade student who scored at the 7th percentile on the fall benchmark screener. The team members confirmed through two other valid measures that Bobby was significantly at risk. As a result, Bobby began receiving a moderately intense 30-minute intervention, 5 days a week. His progress monitoring goal was set using the screening tool's expected grade level ROI of 1.2 words read correctly. After 6 weeks, the team members reconvened and determined that Bobby's actual ROI of 0.7 was well below expectations. Through the DBI process, the team members intensified the intervention, reset the goal using the grade-level ROI, and continued to monitor his progress. After 6 more weeks, the team members reconvened and determined that while Bobby's actual ROI of 0.9 was higher than that in the previous intervention period, it was still below the grade-level ROI of 1.2 words reads read correctly. The team members confirmed the intervention and subsequent adaptations were delivered with fidelity. Two weeks later, Bobby scored at the 4th percentile on the winter benchmark screener and was again confirmed to be significantly at risk.

You and your two to three colleagues are now the new second-grade team. With your team members, discuss the following questions and come to consensus about whether you would recommend that Bobby be referred for special education, providing a rationale for your team's decision:

1. What information from the scenario might suggest a referral is appropriate?
2. What information from the scenario might suggest that there are insufficient data to support a referral?
3. Should the team consider a referral for special education testing? Why or why not?
4. What other next steps might the team recommend?

FREQUENTLY ASKED QUESTIONS

How does DBI fit within MTSS implementation at secondary grades?

Although the components of MTSS at the secondary levels are the same as those found in an elementary MTSS model, the tools and outcomes differ. Intensive intervention is an essential component of MTSS models for older students, and the processes for implementing DBI as part of MTSS still apply. For secondary literacy MTSS models, there is strong evidence for providing individualized, intensive interventions that focus on the knowledge and skills necessary for comprehending complex text (Kamil et al., 2008). Many secondary MTSS models focus on dropout prevention. For these models, evidence has shown that providing intensive intervention designed to support academic, social–emotional, and personal needs can improve outcomes for students identified as being at risk for dropout (Rumberger et al., 2017). DBI has the potential to be a powerful tool in providing secondary MTSS teams with a systematic process for intensifying interventions for students who are not progressing toward literacy or graduation outcomes.

What is necessary for schools to sustain DBI implementation?

To ensure sustained implementation of DBI within an MTSS framework, schools should ensure that the leadership fully supports implementation of the DBI process. This leads to increased staff buy-in and ensures better alignment with MTSS. Formalizing procedures through standard protocols and providing ongoing professional development will increase fidelity to the process and equitable access to DBI for all students. Finally, school teams need to commit to trusting the process. It is important to understand that teams will face challenges along the way and should therefore use processes for systematically addressing problems as they arise.

Why should schools ensure students with disabilities have access to DBI within MTSS?

Many students who require intensive intervention also are students with disabilities. As a result, schools must ensure that students with disabilities have access to DBI as part of the available continuum of services. Under the IDEA, students with disabilities are provided specialized instruction based on the areas of need identified in the IEP. When students with disabilities need more intensive supports, DBI strategies are infused into their special education planning as part of their IEP. Students with disabilities who require DBI are most successful when DBI is implemented as part of MTSS. When DBI is implemented within a larger, schoolwide MTSS model, students with disabilities can receive intensive intervention, while being ensured access to aligned Tier 1 instruction and supports and Tier 2 intervention in other areas of identified need.

What should we do if we have too many students needing intensive intervention?

When more than 3–5% of students are identified as needing intensive instruction, schools should consider strengthening the instruction and behavior supports provided at Tiers 1 and 2. Selecting interventions at Tier 2 that are not likely to produce large performance gains can lead to overidentification of students needing DBI. To avoid this common challenge, select Tier 2 interventions that rate high among the dimensions of intervention intensity and have been shown to improve student outcomes. This will increase the number of students likely to respond to the Tier 2 intervention, thus reducing the number of students needing intensive intervention.

How should schools involve families in decision making for DBI and MTSS?

Involving families in decision-making processes is an essential part of MTSS and DBI implementation. Parents know their child well and can offer school teams valuable information about their child's needs, preferences, and motivators. This information can assist teams in developing more effective individualized behavior and academic intervention plans. When families are provided information about the specific skills and goals toward which their child is working, they can also better support learning at home. To support ongoing collaboration with families, schools should establish communication procedures to ensure that families are informed about the school's approach to MTSS and DBI, have opportunities to share information about their children, and can participate in problem-solving meetings as appropriate.

REFERENCES

Al Otaiba, S., Wagner, R. K., & Miller, B. (2014). "Waiting to fail" redux: Understanding inadequate response to intervention. *Learning Disability Quarterly, 37*(3), 129–133.

Arden, S. V., Gandhi, A., Zumeta Edmonds, R., & Danielson, L. (2017). Toward more effective systems: Lessons from national implementation efforts. *Exceptional Children, 83*(3), 269–280.

Burns, M. K., Appleton, J. J., & Stehouwer, D. J. (2005). Meta-analytic review of responsiveness to intervention research: Examining field-based and research implemented models. *Journal of Psychoeducational Assessment, 23*, 381–394.

Center on Response to Intervention. (2010). *Essential components of RTI: A closer look at response to intervention.* Washington, DC: U.S. Department of Education, Office of Special Education Programs, National Center on Response to Intervention.

Center on Response to Intervention. (2012). *RTI implementer series: Module 1. Screening.* Washington, DC: U.S. Department of Education, Office of Special Education Programs, National Center on Response to Intervention.

Danielson, L., & Rosenquist, C. (2014). Introduction to the TEC special issue on data-based individualization. *TEACHING Exceptional Children, 46*(4), 6–12.

Dexter, D. D., Hughes, C. A., & Farmer T. W. (2008). Response to intervention: A review of field studies and implication for rural special education. *Rural Special Education Quarterly, 27*, 3–9.

Fuchs, D., Compton, D. L., Fuchs, L. S., Bryant, J., & Davis, N. G. (2008). Making "secondary intervention" work in a three-tier responsiveness-to-intervention model: Findings from the first-grade longitudinal reading study of the National Research Center on Learning Disabilities. *Reading and Writing Quarterly: An Interdisciplinary Journal, 21*(4), 413–436.

Fuchs, D., & Fuchs, L. S. (1998). Researchers and teachers working together to adapt instruction for diverse learners. *Learning Disabilities Research and Practice, 13*, 126–137.

Fuchs, D., Fuchs, L., & Compton, D. (2012). Smart RTI: A next-generation approach to multi-level prevention. *Exceptional Children, 78*(3), 263–279.

Fuchs, D., Mock, D., Morgan, P. L., & Young, C. (2003). Responsiveness-to-intervention: Definitions, evidence, and implications for the learning disabilities construct. *Learning Disabilities Research and Practice, 18*, 157–171.

Gandhi, A. G., Vaughn, S., Stelitano, L., Scala, J., & Danielson, L. (2015). Lessons learned from district implementation of intensive intervention: A focus on students with disabilities. *Journal of Special Education Leadership, 28*(1), 39–49.

Hughes, C., & Dexter, D. D. (2015). The use of RTI to identify students with learning disabilities:

A review of the research. Retrieved from *www.rtinetwork.org/learn/research/use-rti-identify-students-learning-disabilities-review-research.*

Kamil, M. L., Borman, G. D., Dole, J., Kral, C. C., Salinger, T., & Torgesen, J. (2008). *Improving adolescent literacy: Effective classroom and intervention practices: A practice guide* (NCEE #2008-4027). Washington, DC: National Center for Education Evaluation and Regional Assistance, Institute of Education Sciences, U.S. Department of Education.

Memorandum to State Directors of Special Education, 56 IDELR 50 (Office of Special Education Programs 2011). Retrieved from *https://www2.ed.gov/policy/speced/guid/idea/memosdcltrs/osep11-07rtimemo.pdf.*

National Center on Intensive Intervention. (2013a). *Implementing intensive intervention: Lessons learned from the field.* Washington, DC: U.S. Department of Education, Office of Special Education Programs.

National Center on Intensive Intervention. (2013b, July). *Introduction to data-based individualization (DBI): Considerations for implementation in academics and behavior.* Washington, DC: U.S. Department of Education, Office of Special Education Programs, National Center on Intensive Intervention.

National Center on Intensive Intervention. (2018). Intensive intervention and multi-tiered systems of support (MTSS). Retrieved from *https://intensiveintervention.org/intensive-intervention/multi-tiered-systems-support.*

Ruffini, S. J., Lindsay, J., McInerney, M., Waite, W., & Miskell, R. (2016). *Measuring the implementation fidelity of the Response to Intervention framework in Milwaukee Public Schools* (REL 2017-192). Washington, DC: U.S. Department of Education, Institute of Education Sciences, National Center for Education Evaluation and Regional Assistance, Regional Educational Laboratory Midwest. Retrieved from *http://ies.ed.gov/ncee/edlabss.*

Rumberger, R., Addis, H., Allensworth, E., Balfanz, R., Bruch, J., Dillon, E., . . . Tuttle, C. (2017). *Preventing dropout in secondary schools* (NCEE 2017-4028). Washington, DC: National Center for Education Evaluation and Regional Assistance (NCEE), Institute of Education Sciences, U.S. Department of Education.

Stecker, P. M., Fuchs, L. S., & Fuchs, D. (2005). Using curriculum-based measurement to improve student achievement: Review of research. *Psychology in the Schools, 42*(8), 795–819.

VanDerHeyden, A. M., Witt, J. C., & Gilbertson, D. (2007). A multi-year evaluation of the effects of a response to intervention (RTI) model on identification of children for special education. *Journal of School Psychology, 45,* 225–256.

Wehby, J. (2013). Ask the expert: For students with intensive behavior needs, how many data points are needed to make decisions? Retrieved from *https://intensiveintervention.org/resource/providing-intensive-intervention-using-data-based-individualization-behavior.*

Data-Based Individualization Implementation Log:
Daily and Weekly Intervention Review

Purpose: This log can be used as a daily and weekly record of your implementation of an individual student's intensive intervention plan. This information, along with progress monitoring graphs, can inform team intervention and data review meetings. To review implementation of the data-based individualization (DBI) process for this student, also see the *Student-Level Data-Based Individualization Implementation Checklists*.

Teacher: _____

Student: _____

Week of: _____

Daily Intervention Log

Please fill out this log each day. If an intervention is not scheduled for a given day or could not be offered (e.g., holiday, your absence), then please mark "N" under the column "Intervention Offered?" and leave the rest of the row blank. On days when the student receives intervention (Student Present? = Y), indicate the duration (minutes) or frequency (e.g., number of check-ins) of the intervention, rate the extent of student engagement, and rate the plan implementation.

Day	Intervention Offered	Student Present	Intervention Duration or Frequency	Was the Student Engaged *No Partially Yes*	Was the Intervention Implemented as Planned *No Partially Yes*
Monday	☐ Y ☐ N	☐ Y ☐ N		☐ 1 ☐ 2 ☐ 3	☐ 1 ☐ 2 ☐ 3
Tuesday	☐ Y ☐ N	☐ Y ☐ N		☐ 1 ☐ 2 ☐ 3	☐ 1 ☐ 2 ☐ 3
Wednesday	☐ Y ☐ N	☐ Y ☐ N		☐ 1 ☐ 2 ☐ 3	☐ 1 ☐ 2 ☐ 3
Thursday	☐ Y ☐ N	☐ Y ☐ N		☐ 1 ☐ 2 ☐ 3	☐ 1 ☐ 2 ☐ 3
Friday	☐ Y ☐ N	☐ Y ☐ N		☐ 1 ☐ 2 ☐ 3	☐ 1 ☐ 2 ☐ 3

Please note any relevant information to explain the above ratings.

(continued)

Data-Based Individualization Implementation Log (page 2 of 2)

End-of-Week Evaluation

Implementation

Reflecting on your daily ratings, please rate overall implementation this week.

	No	Partially	Yes
Did you implement the **intervention plan** as intended this week?	☐ 1	☐ 2	☐ 3
Did you implement the **data collection plan** as intended this week?	☐ 1	☐ 2	☐ 3

If you selected a 1 or 2 for either of the above items, then please note what occurred, including any intervention adaptations that were not in the plan. Also, please note any additional relevant information.

Need for Further Adaptation

Do student data indicate the need for an adaptation to the intervention based on predetermined decision rules?

☐ Yes

☐ No

Does the plan need to be changed due to barriers to implementation (the schedule does not allow sufficient time, staff need more training, etc.)?

☐ Yes

☐ No

If an adaptation is needed ("Yes" to either question above), then consider the following: What level of adaptation is needed to improve your plan for next week?

☐ Minor

☐ Major

Do you need to meet with the team before moving forward with the adaptation?

☐ Yes

☐ No

Next Week's Action Plan

Please describe any planned modifications for next week.

Glossary

Aimline: Sometimes referred to as the *goal line,* the aimline represents the target rate of student progress over time on a progress monitoring assessment graph. The aimline is constructed by connecting the data point representing the student's initial performance level and the data point corresponding to the student's final goal. The aimline should be compared to the *trendline* to help inform responsiveness to intervention and to tailor a student's instructional program.

Alternative and augmentative communication (AAC) specialist: A professional who teaches individuals with verbal impairments to communicate using low-tech (e.g., picture icons) and high-tech (e.g., speech-generating) devices.

Antecedent: Within the context of functional behavior assessment, antecedents are events that occur before a target behavior.

Behavior: Within the context of functional behavior assessment, behavior is a measurable action. A target behavior is whatever is considered the most important thing to change.

Behavioral generalization: Performing a behavior in a different manner or setting than the context in which it was learned.

Capacity building: The process of developing and building knowledge, skills, and processes related to a given innovation or practice.

Child Find: The component of the Individual with Disabilities Education Act that requires states to develop and implement a practical method for determining which children with disabilities are receiving special education and related services and which children are not.

Consequence: Within the context of functional behavior assessment, a consequence refers to the event or events that immediately follow the target behavior.

Content expert: An individual with training and expertise in specific content areas, such as behavior support or literacy. The content expert has an understanding of the research base for the content area, has experience in delivering the content with students, and has supported staff members who work with students in the specific content.

Curriculum-based measurement (CBM): A form of standardized, general outcome progress monitoring that is intended to guide instructional decision making. CBM assessments can systematically sample the curriculum, or they can rely on a single behavior that functions as an overall indicator of competence in an academic area.

Cut point: The score on the test below which students are deemed at-risk for poor long-term outcomes in that academic domain.

Data-based decision making: The ongoing process of analyzing and evaluating student data to inform educational decisions, including, but not limited to, approaches to instruction, intervention, allocation of resources, development of policy, movement within a multilevel system, and disability identification.

Data-based individualization (DBI): A systematic, iterative, multistep approach to intensive intervention that involves the ongoing analysis of progress monitoring and diagnostic data, followed by intensification and individualization of validated academic and/or behavioral intervention programs.

Developmental disability (DD): A broad term that includes autism spectrum disorders, cerebral palsy, and other disorders that occur during the developmental period.

Diagnostic assessment: A type of assessment intended to identify a student's strengths and weaknesses related to specific content areas, skills, or strategies.

Diagnostic data: Data that may be used to identify a student's specific skills deficits and strengths. Data may be derived from standardized measures, error analysis of progress monitoring data, student work samples, and behavior rating forms, among other tools.

Direct behavior rating (DBR): A behavior progress monitoring method that combines aspects of behavior rating scales (teacher rating) and direct observation (recording right after the intervention period and repeated administration). The term DBR outlines the central features of the method. Specifically, DBR is Direct (ratings are collected immediately after the observation period), targets Behavior (rates behaviors such as Academic Engagement, Disruptive Behavior, and Respectful), and involves Rating (based on the rater's perception of the target behavior).

Down syndrome: A genetic disorder caused by the presence of all or part of a third copy of chromosome 21. This most common genetic cause of intellectual disability is also known as trisomy 21.

Effect size: A statistical measure of the magnitude of the relationship between two variables. Within education, an effect size often represents the magnitude of the relationship between participating in an intervention and an academic or behavioral outcome of interest. The larger the effect size, the greater the impact that participating in the intervention had on the outcome.

Escape: Within the context of functional behavior assessment, a consequence that maintains a target behavior by allowing the student to avoid some undesirable situation or outcome.

Evidence-based intervention: An intervention for which data from scientific, rigorous research studies have demonstrated (or empirically validated) the efficacy of the intervention. Applying findings from experimental studies, single-case studies, or strong quasi-experimental studies, an evidence-based intervention improves student learning beyond what would be expected without that intervention. An evidence-based intervention may also be known as a *validated intervention.*

False positive: Students mistakenly identified as being at risk based on performance on a screening assessment.

Fidelity of implementation: The implementation of a practice or program as intended by the researchers or developers. Also known as *treatment integrity* or *procedural fidelity.*

Full implementation: When an innovation, initiative, program, or process becomes fully ingrained into the business-as-usual practice within an organization such as a school. Full implementation of any schoolwide initiative often takes multiple years to occur.

Functional behavior assessment: A diagnostic approach that identifies the function of behavior (i.e., why the behavior is occurring).

General outcome measure (GOM): A progress monitoring measure that simultaneously assesses performance across the many skills represented in the annual curriculum. These measures are standardized, have a long-term focus, so that testing methods and content remain consistent, and are usually fluency based.

Individualized education program (IEP): A legal document that describes the plan for delivering specially designed instruction, related services, and accommodations to meet the educational needs of a student with a disability.

Initial implementation: The period when implementation of an innovation, initiative, program, or process begins. This is when the most systems-level changes are required by the organization implementing the new practice.

Intellectual disability (ID): Individuals with intellectual disability have an IQ that is 2 standard deviations below the mean (e.g., 70 or lower) and significant limitations in adaptive behaviors, both of which occurred prior to the age of 18 years.

Intervention adaptation: Teachers use data (including progress monitoring and diagnostic data) to revise, modify, intensify, or individualize an intervention to target a student's specific needs. Strategies for intensifying an intervention may occur along several dimensions—including, but not limited to, changes to group size, frequency, or duration; or changes to the instructional principles incorporated within the intervention or in providing feedback.

Intervention team: A group of building-level staff members who are responsible for intervention-related decisions, including, but not limited to, placement within tiers, intervention adaptations, data analysis, and progress monitoring. This often includes a building administrator, school psychologist, intervention staff, special education teacher, and instructional coach or specialist.

Interventionist: The individual who provides intervention to a student. An interventionist may provide support in academics, behavior, or both content areas. The interventionist may be the classroom teacher, special education service provider, paraprofessional, or others as identified by the student support team or IEP team.

Learning lab: Space where students with disabilities at the secondary school level can go during a particular class period to work with a special education or general education teacher. In some schools, this is an elective for the student; in other cases, it is part of the student's course plan.

Line of best fit: The line drawn through data points when a student's progress monitoring scores are graphed against time; the slope of this line is calculated to quantify the student's rate of learning.

Mastery measure: A progress monitoring measure that assesses mastery of a sequence of skills. A mastery measurement progress monitoring system is characterized by a hierarchy of skills for instruction and a criterion-referenced test for each skill in the instructional hierarchy.

Multilevel prevention system: A system that provides access to increasingly intense levels of instruction and interventions. It typically includes three levels of intensity or prevention: primary, secondary, and intensive prevention. These levels are sometimes also called Tier 1, Tier 2, and Tier 3.

Multi-tiered system of support (MTSS): A prevention framework that organizes building-level resources to address each individual student's academic and/or behavioral needs within intervention tiers that vary in intensity. MTSS allows for the early identification of learning and behavioral challenges, and timely intervention for students who are at risk for poor learning outcomes. It also may be called a *multilevel prevention system.* The increasingly intense tiers (e.g., Tier 1, Tier 2, Tier 3), sometimes referred to as *levels of prevention* (i.e., primary, secondary, intensive prevention levels), represent a continuum of supports. Response to intervention (RTI) and positive behavioral interventions and supports (PBIS) are examples of MTSS.

Positive behavioral interventions and supports (PBIS): A tiered behavior support framework for enhancing the adoption and implementation of a continuum of evidence-based interventions to achieve behaviorally important outcomes for all students. PBIS provides a data-driven decision-making framework that guides the selection, integration, and implementation of preventive and instructive behavioral practices.

Positive reinforcement: The addition of a consequence that increases the likelihood that the target behavior will increase by resulting in some desired outcome.

Progress monitoring: Repeated measurement of student performance over the course of intervention to index and quantify responsiveness to intervention and to thus determine, on an ongoing basis, when adjustments to the program are needed to improve responsiveness. Progress monitoring is used to assess a student's performance, to quantify his or her rate of improvement or responsiveness to intervention, to adjust the student's instructional program to make it more effective and suited to the student's needs, and to evaluate the effectiveness of the intervention.

Referral: Under the Individual with Disabilities Education Act, a referral begins the formal process of determining eligibility for special education services.

Reinforcement: A consequence that increases the likelihood that a behavior will occur in the future.

Response to intervention (RTI): A framework that integrates assessment and intervention within a multilevel prevention system to maximize student achievement and reduce behavior problems. With RTI, schools identify students at risk for poor learning outcomes; monitor student progress; provide evidence-based interventions, and adjust the intensity and nature of those interventions depending on a student's responsiveness; and identify students with learning disabilities or other disabilities.

Screening: Assessment designed to identify students at risk for poor learning outcomes.

Second-stage screening: The process of following up universal screening (the brief tests administered to everyone in the school) with a second round of screening assessment using a different, individually administered test for the subset of students who are suspected of being at risk via universal screening.

Slope: An estimate of rate of progress when a student's scores are graphed against time (with progress monitoring this is often weekly or monthly).

Speech–language pathologist (SLP): A professional who evaluates and treats patients with speech, language, cognitive-communication, and swallowing disorders in individuals of all ages, from infants to elderly adults. In schools, SLPs often provide support around speech, communication, language, and literacy.

Standardized agenda: A structured meeting outline that provides a predictable process and is followed consistently during each meeting.

Sustainability: The extent to which an initiative, program, or process is maintained over time.

Systematic direct observation (SDO): A behavior assessment method in which an observer records operationally defined target behavior(s) using a specific coding framework, including a time sampling strategy (e.g., momentary time sampling).

Taxonomy of intervention intensity: A systematic approach to intensifying an intervention. The taxonomy comprises seven dimensions: strength, dosage, alignment, attention to transfer, comprehensiveness, behavioral or academic support, and individualization.

Tier 1: Also known as *primary prevention* or *core program,* this first level in a multilevel prevention system should consist of a high-quality core curriculum and research-based instructional practices that meet the needs of most students.

Tier 2: Also known as the *secondary prevention level* or *targeted intervention,* Tier 2 is the second level of intensity in a multilevel prevention system. Interventions occurring at Tier 2 are evidence based and address the learning or behavioral challenges of students identified as being at risk for poor learning or behavioral outcomes.

Tier 3: Also known as *intensive intervention,* Tier 3 is typically the most intense level of a multilevel prevention system. Tier 3 consists of individualized, intensive intervention(s) for students who have severe and persistent learning or behavioral needs, including students with disabilities. Data-based individualization is an approach that may be used within Tier 3.

Index